VEGAN INSTANT POT COOKBOOK

5 Ingredients or Less - Quick, Easy, and Healthy Plant Based Meals for Your Family

Brandon Parker

© Copyright 2017 by –Brandon Parker- All rights reserved.

The following book is reproduced below with the goal of providing information that is as accurate and reliable as possible. Regardless, purchasing this book can be seen as consent to the fact that both the publisher and the author of this book are in no way experts on the topics discussed within and that any recommendations or suggestions that are made herein are for entertainment purposes only. Professionals should be consulted as needed prior to undertaking any of the action endorsed herein.

This declaration is deemed fair and valid by both the American Bar Association and the Committee of Publishers Association and is legally binding throughout the United States.

Furthermore, the transmission, duplication or reproduction of any of the following work including specific information will be considered an illegal act irrespective of if it is done electronically or in print. This extends to creating a secondary or tertiary copy of the work or a recorded copy and is only allowed with express written consent from the Publisher. All additional right reserved.

The information in the following pages is broadly considered to be a truthful and accurate account of facts and as such any inattention, use or misuse of the information in question by the reader will render any resulting actions solely under their purview. There are no scenarios in which the publisher or the original author of this work can be in any fashion deemed liable for any hardship or damages that may befall them after undertaking information described herein.

Additionally, the information in the following pages is intended only for informational purposes and should thus be thought of as universal. As befitting its nature, it is presented without assurance regarding its prolonged validity or interim quality. Trademarks that are mentioned are done without written consent and can in no way be considered an endorsement from the trademark holder.

Contents

Introduction 1
Chapter 1. Basics Functions of the Instant Pot 2
   Different Ways of Using the Instant Pot 8
Chapter 2. Breakfast Options 11
Grain-based options 11
   Champorado (Chocolate Rice Porridge) 11
   Easy Mushroom Congee, Slow Cooked 13
   Granola Overnight Oatmeal, Slow Cooked 15
   Mushroom and Barley Risotto 16
   Pumpkin Flavored Steel Cut Oats 18
   Teff Porridge with Fresh Bananas and Peaches, Sugar-Free 19
Grain-free options 21
   Cassava Mash 21
   Homemade Coconut Butter 22
   Nutty Quinoa with Squash 23
   Potato Squeakers 24
   Savory Sweet Potato Mash 26
   Sweet Hominy with Coconut Flakes 27
   Vanilla Quinoa with Almond Meal 29
Chapter 3. Easy and Quick Lunch Selections 31
Salads and Sandwiches 31
   Breadless Pizza with Squash Flower Toppings 31
   Vegan-Safe Extremely Garlicky Basil Pesto 33
   Homemade Vegan Parmesan Cheese 34
   Horta (Steamed Spinach with Lemon Juice) 35
   Lemon and Soy Portobello Mushrooms 37
   Millet and Zucchini Salad 38
   Spicy Mushroom and Rice Burrito Filling 39
   Warm Potato Salad 40

Tomato Rice Dishes 41
    Basic Tomato Rice 41
    Black Beans, Corn, Tomato in Brown Rice 42
    Black Olives in Tomato Rice 43
    Black Rice with Green Onions 44
    Homemade Mushroom Stock 45
    Homemade Vegetable Stock 47
    Chickpea and Tomato Rice 49
    One Pot Java Rice 50

Chapter 4. Family Dinners and Main Courses 51

Risotto and pasta dishes 51
    Barley and Beetroot Risotto 51
    Easy Barley and Mushroom Risotto 53
    Lemony Asparagus Risotto 54
    Milk and Macaroni Soup 55
    Mushroom Stroganoff, Slow Cooked 56
    Pumpkin in Tagliatelle 57

Soups and Stews 58
    Butternut Squash Soup with Almonds 58
    Chunky Lentil and Tomato Soup 60
    Easy Miso Soup with Tteokbokki 61
    Mushrooms in Vermicelli Noodle Soup 63
    Spiced Hominy Stew 64
    White Beans and Kale Stew 65

Chapter 5. Desserts and Sweets 66

Filling desserts 66
    Creamy Sweet Potato Mash 66
    Palitaw (Rice Ball Patties with Coconut Flakes and Sesame Seeds) ... 68
    Stewed Apples with Walnuts 69
    Sweet Chickpeas in Almond Milk (No Pre-Soaking) 71
    Taho (Silken Tofu with Tapioca Pearls) 72

Ube Halaya (Purple Yam Mash) 73
Short and sweet (cooks in 20 minutes or less) 74
    Boiled Plantains 74
    Bubur Cha Cha (Root Crops Stewed in Coconut Cream) 75
    Chocolate Raspberry Pudding with Chia Seeds 76
    Kluai Buad Chi (Almond Milk Stewed Bananas) 77
    Orange-Scented Tapioca Pearls 78
    Steamed Peanut Butter Cups 79
Chapter 6. Bread and Savory Snacks 80
Easy bread recipes 80
    Baozi (Steamed Buns) Filled with Mushroom Stroganoff 80
    Crockpot Bread Loaf, Slow Cooked 82
    Easy No-Bake Flatbread 84
    Garlic Beer Pita Bread 85
    Putong Bigas (Steamed Rice Cakes) 86
    Ube Puto (Steamed Purple Yam Cakes) 87
Vegetable-based 88
    Aloo Pakora (Potato Fritters) 88
    Boiled Edamame in Pods 90
    Boiled Peanuts 91
    Corn on the Cob with Coconut Butter 92
    Corn Pakora (Sweet Corn Fritters) 93
    Flavored Vinegar 94
    Pinakurat 94
    Sinamak 95
    Salty and Sweet Chickpeas 96
Conclusion 98

Introduction

Thank you for getting a copy of, "*Vegan Instant Pot Cookbook: 5 Ingredients or Less - Quick, Easy, and Healthy Plant Based Meals for Your Family.*"

Despite common misconception, vegan cooking is exciting, flavorsome, and not that complicated to make from scratch. Vegan meals are healthier than most meat-based dishes because most ingredients are organically low in cholesterol, fat, and sugar. These are a boon to people who are trying to cut back on calories, those who are trying to control their blood sugar and cholesterol levels, and those who want to introduce their children to more fresh fruits and vegetables.

With the help of the **Instant Pot** and its numerous cooking functions, healthy vegan dishes can be prepared, cooked, and served in less than an hour, and with only five ingredients (or less!)

The **Instant Pot** is a versatile machine. It can braise, boil, pressure cook, sauté, shallow-fry, slow cook, and steam dishes all in one pot. It can cook everything from simple porridges, to quick savory snacks, and even desserts.

This book contains 60+ vegan-safe recipes for breakfast, lunch, and dinner. These include everything from grain-based breakfast options, to easy soups, and to stick-to-your-ribs dinner selections. There are also healthy choices for those who love to munch on savory snacks in between meals, and those who love to give in to their sweet tooth.

In the interest of good health, recipes within will include mostly fresh and whole food. Small amount of processed food is utilized, like: canned mushrooms, dried beans, non-dairy based milk, tofu, etc.

This book also contains tips on how to: buy ingredients without spending a lot of money, prepare/cook ingredients properly for maximum flavor, prepare/cook dishes with minimal fuss, substitute ingredients to create variations of same dish, and where to find exotic ingredients.

Lastly, this book contains information on how to use the **Instant Pot** properly, in case this is your first time using this machine, or you would like to know a few tricks to amplify the use of this cooker.

Thanks again for getting a copy of this book. I hope you enjoy it.

Chapter 1. Basics Functions of the Instant Pot

It should be noted immediately that recipes included in this book are all for **Instant Pots** that have six liters (and more) capacities. When using smaller machines, adjust volume of food accordingly to prevent overflows.[1]

There are currently three kinds of **Instant Pots** in the market: DUO, LUX and SMART. Buttons may be in different positions or renamed, but these almost have the same functions. Namely:

- **Bean / Chili.** Use this function to cook dishes at **high pressure** for **30 minutes**. Heat setting can be changed by pressing either the **Adjust** or **Manual** button or the [+] or [-] buttons. Automatically prolonged or shortened to **40 minutes** and **25 minutes**, respectively by pressing the **Adjust** button once or twice.

- **Meat / Stew.** Some models only have **Meat** options, while others only have **Stew** options. Use said function to cook dishes at **high pressure** for **35 minutes**. Automatically prolonged or shortened to **45 minutes** and **20 minutes**, respectively by pressing the **Adjust** button once or twice. Despite being labeled as **Meat**, this function can also be used when cooking vegan dishes.

- **Multigrain.** Use this function to cook dishes at **high pressure** for **40 minutes**. Automatically prolonged or shortened to **45 minutes** and **25 minutes**, respectively by pressing the **Adjust** button once or twice. Although technically different, this function cooks both

---

[1] When using other brands, check for psi (pressure per square inch.) **Instant Pot** cooks at 11 psi. If machines you are using have higher psi, shorten cooking time; for lower psi, lengthen cooking time.

multigrain[2] and wholegrain[3] (e.g. barley pearls, millet, and wild rice, etc.) preferably with lots of liquids.

- **Porridge.** Use this function to cook dishes at **high pressure** for **20 minutes**. Automatically prolonged or shortened to **30 minutes** and **15 minutes**, respectively by pressing the **Adjust** button once or twice. This is best used for dishes with faster cooking grains like: bulgur or cracked wheat, oats, quinoa and white rice.

- **Poultry.** Use this function to cook dishes at **high pressure** for **15 minutes**. Automatically prolonged or shortened to **30 minutes** and **5 minutes**, respectively by pressing the **Adjust** button once or twice. Aside from cooking chicken cutlets, use this function for cooking roots crops in water like: sweet potatoes and taro. This is not recommended when cooking whole chicken.

- **Pressure** (pressure cooker.) Pressure plus heat make it easier and faster to cook relatively tough ingredients. This reduces cooking time to a quarter, as compared to oven or stovetop cooking. This function defaults to low pressure, but can be overridden for high pressure. Cooking time must be manually keyed. After sealing the lid, turn the knob on top to **Sealing**.

  When preheated, the **Instant Pot** usually comes to the desired pressure in ten to twenty seconds. When cooking cold, it takes a maximum of two minutes. This is faster than stovetop pressure cookers that come to pressure only after twenty minutes, or five minutes after liquids inside the pot come to a rolling boil.

  It's unsafe to open the cooker's lid when there's a lot of internal pressure, which is why many stovetop pressure cookers explode or send their lids flying into the ceiling when prematurely opened.

  Fortunately, with the **Instant Pot**, there are safety precautions that prevent users from prematurely opening the lid. These include two safety releases: **natural pressure release** and **quick pressure release**.

  - **Natural pressure release** is when the machine depressurizes on its own. Depending on the volume of liquid inside, this could take between **8 to 30 minutes**. The valve on the **Instant Pot** lid must remain in the **Sealing** position always.

---

[2] A combination of different types of grains.
[3] A single type of grain is used.

It is almost impossible to open the lid during this time. When the machine starts beeping, it means that the pressure within the crockpot has subsided. That would be the perfect time to carefully open the lid. Steam would still be present because the dish inside is piping hot. Either turn off the machine immediately, or let the machine automatically switch to **Warm** mode.

- o **Quick pressure release** is when pressure is gradually released by opening the release valve on the lid. Simply turn the knob from **Sealing** to **Venting**. Depending on the volume of liquid inside, this process can take as little as 2 minutes or as much as 14 minutes.

  Make sure machine is nowhere near overhead cupboards of expensive fixtures. Steam coming out from the lid can damage these. Wait for the steam to stop streaming. The machine will start beeping when it's safe to open the lid. Either turn off the machine immediately, or let the machine automatically switch to **Warm** mode.

  NOTE: **Instant Pot** has a **Cancel** option. When cancelling any dish during pressure cooking, always opt for **quick pressure release** immediately after. Do not unplug the machine before doing so. This will only make it harder to reopen the crockpot's lid. Forcing the lid open with high pressure within will only damage the machine's mechanism and void product warranty.

- **Rice** or **rice cooker**. This is the only fully automatic function. After rinsing rice and pouring in recommended amount of water, press this function and seal the lid. Rice will cook at **low pressure**. An internal mechanism will adjust cooking time depending on the volume of liquid still in the crockpot after a certain time. This is a good example of set-the-machine-and-walk-away type of cooking. Even when rice is overwatered, the machine will automatically adjust.

Rice can also be cooked faster using the **pressure cooker** function. The difference in cooking time (as compared to the rice cooking function) is only between **5 and 10 minutes**. Specific and precise instructions must be keyed in prior to cooking. The machine cannot rectify any mistakes during cooking. When cooking large volumes of rice, always opt for the preset **rice cooker** function to avoid overcooking or undercooking rice.

- **Sauté.** Use this function to stir-fry aromatics and to brown ingredients prior to stewing. This can also be used to shallow-fry vegetables. Always keep lid **off** when sautéing. This function should not be used for deep frying.

  Press sauté button to simmer dishes. Keep lid on but do not seal. This makes it easier to check if the dish is not drying out too quickly.

  If this function is used a lot when cooking, it's highly recommended to buy a separate **Instant Pot** aluminum lid. This is lighter in construction than the standard lid. Choose one that fits the crockpot's size.

  Heat setting for this function can be adjusted in some **Instant Pot** models. Press either **Adjust** or **Manual** button once for browning (high heat,) and twice for simmering (low heat.)

- **Slow cook** or **slow cooker.** Use this function for slow braising. This is especially useful when relatively tougher ingredients, or when cooking grains so that these break down completely.

  With all models, this function defaults to **4 hours** at **low pressure** or at 190°F to 201°F (87°C to 94°C.) But this can be overridden to prolong/shorten cooking time or to increase cooking temperature to 199°F to 210°F (93°C to 99°C) using either the **Adjust** or **Manual** buttons.

- **Soup.** Use this function to cook dishes at **high pressure** for **30 minutes**. Automatically prolonged or shortened to **40 minutes** and **20 minutes**, respectively by pressing the **Adjust** button once or twice. Soups make great one-pot meals when chosen ingredients finish cooking at the same time.

Due to the relatively larger volume of liquid used in making soups, these can be cooked at **low pressure** and allow to stay at **Warm** mode for a long time.

For hectic days, pour ingredients into crockpot and seal lid. Program timer to go off an hour or two after leaving the house. By which time, dish will start cooking on its own. By lunch time, dish will be ready to serve, without overcooking the ingredients. Or, delay cooking time to four to five hours when preparing dinner.

- **Steam.** Some **Instant Pot** models come with stainless steel steaming rack/trivet or with steam rack basket set. Use this for steaming food at **high pressure** for **10 minutes**. Automatically prolonged or shortened to **15 minutes** and **3 minutes**, respectively by pressing the **Adjust** button once or twice.

  In case **Instant Pot** model doesn't come with its own steaming accessory, use suitable-sized bamboo steamers.

- **Yogurt.** This is often used to ferment milk into yogurt, usually in a succession of cooking steps, e.g. warming the milk, cultivating milk with yogurt starters, etc. For this function, it is highly recommended to follow the instructions in the product guide specific to the **Instant Pot** model.

  This should not be used for canning or for sterilizing bottles or containers.

Other functions:

- **Adjust** and/or **Manual**. Some models only have an **Adjust** button, others only have a **Manual** button. There's also models that have separate **Adjust** and **Manual** buttons, with the former also serving as the **On/Off** button.

  In any case, this/these is/are multi-function button(s.) If not using any of the set functions, press said button(s) to override existing programs. For example: when slow cooking, press either the **Adjust** or **Manual** button to increase or decrease cooking temperature, and/or prolong or shorten cooking time.

  To make cooking instructions clearer though, this book will address functions of these buttons separately.

- **Keep Warm (Warm) / Cancel**. With some models, this is labeled as: **Warm / Cancel**. If for any reason, cooking functions must be stopped, this is the go-to button. Press once or twice until display window clears or goes back to **On**. Press desired cooking function and cooking time afterwards.

Keep Warm function automatically kicks into gear after each cooking cycle. As long as machine is plugged in, the dish inside (preferably something with lots of liquids like soups and stews) will remain hot or warm and ready to serve. Turn off machine immediately when cooking relatively dry dishes.

The warming temperature in the **Instant Pot** SMART machine can be manually adjusted.

- Plus and minus buttons, [+] and [-]. After pressing the **Adjust** or **Manual** buttons, choose either one to increase or decrease cooking temperature or time accordingly.

- **Timer**. Use to delay cooking, preferably for dishes with lots of liquids, like soups and stews. This is not recommended for dishes that burn quickly or relative dry.

Key in cooking functions first, and then cooking time. Press **Timer** button, and then press the [+] or [-] buttons depending on when you want the machine to start cooking (e.g. after an hour or after four hours.)

Do not press this button when adjusting cooking time for other functions. Use the **Adjust** or **Manual** button instead, and then the [+] or [-] buttons.

Different Ways of Using the Instant Pot[4]

A.
1. After preparing ingredients, pour these into the crockpot. This is the inner metal sleeve of the cooker. For the sake of brevity, this will be referred to henceforth as **crockpot**.
2. Seal lid. Turn lid knob to **sealing**.
3. Press desired function, e.g. **rice cooker**.
4. Wait for the machine to automatically start cooking, and then switch to **Warm / Keep Warm** after cooking cycle. There is no need to stay in the kitchen when the machine is running.
5. Remove lid. Turn off machine. Serve food.

B.
1. After preparing ingredients, pour these into the crockpot.
2. Seal lid. Turn lid knob to **sealing**.
3. Press desired function, e.g. **slow cooker**.
4. Press **manual** once (or twice, depending on machine) to shift cooker from **low pressure** to **high pressure**. Light will show up in the display window what heat setting you are using.

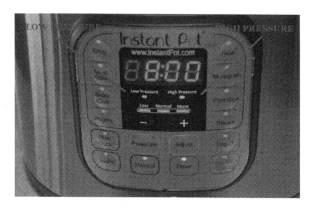

5. Key in preferred cooking time.
6. Wait for the machine to automatically start cooking, and then switch to **Warm / Keep Warm** after cooking cycle.
7. Remove lid. Turn off machine. Serve.

---

[4] When in doubt, check machine's product booklet.

C.
1. Prepare ingredients. Press **sauté** on the **Instant Pot**. Remove lid.
2. Wait for base of crockpot to heat up before pouring in aromatics, which should include some form of oil (e.g. coconut or olive oil.)
3. Stir-fry aromatics until cooked to desired doneness.
4. Add in remaining ingredients either in succession or all in. Stir as needed.
5. Seal lid. Turn lid knob to sealing.
6. Press desired function, e.g. **soup**.
7. Press **timer**, and then [+] or [-] button to delay cooking time by three (or more) hours.
8. Wait for machine to automatically start cooking, and then switch to **Keep Warm (Warm)** after cooking cycle.
9. Remove lid. Turn off machine. Serve.

D.
1. Prepare ingredients. Press **sauté** on the **Instant Pot**. Remove lid.
2. Wait for base of crockpot to heat up before pouring in aromatics, which should include some form of oil (e.g. coconut or olive oil.)
3. Stir-fry aromatics until cooked to desired doneness.
4. Add in remaining ingredients either in succession or all in. Stir as needed.
5. Seal lid. Turn lid knob to **sealing**.
6. Press desired function, e.g. **pressure cooker**.
7. Press **manual**, and choose **high pressure**.
8. **Adjust** cooking time to desired length, e.g. **30 minutes**.
9. Wait for the machine to automatically start cooking, and then switch to **Warm / Keep Warm** after cooking cycle.
10. Choose **quick pressure release** by turning lid knob to **venting**. Wait for steam to subside. Remove lid. Turn off machine.
11. Ladle/spoon portions into bowls/plates. Add garnishes, if any. Serve.

E.
1. Prepare ingredients. Place ingredients into steamer-safe containers, e.g. dumplings into bamboo steaming baskets.
2. Place steaming rack into bottom of crockpot. Place steaming basket on top.
3. Pour in recommended amount of water. As a safety precaution, always add at least a cup of water into crockpot when steaming
4. Seal lid. Turn lid knob to **sealing**.
5. Press **steam** on the **Instant Pot**.

6. Wait for the machine to automatically start cooking, and then switch to **Warm / Keep Warm** after cooking cycle.
7. Remove lid. Turn off machine. Serve.

Chapter 2. Breakfast Options

Grain-based options

Champorado (Chocolate Rice Porridge)

Prep Time: 10 minutes; **Cook Time**: 7 minutes
Recommended Serving Size: 1 cup; **Serves**: 4

Ingredients:
- 4½ cups water
- ¾ cup brown rice, rinsed, drained
- ½ cup vegan-safe chocolate buttons, plus 1 Tbsp. for garnish, divided
- ¼ cup light coconut milk, divided
- ½ Tbsp. brown sugar, add more if desired

Directions:
1. Reserve a tablespoon of chocolate buttons and light coconut milk as garnishes. Divide into 4 equal portions. Chill in fridge until needed.
2. Except for remaining chocolate buttons, stir in remaining ingredients into crockpot.
3. Close lid and lock. Lid knob should be at **sealing**.
4. Press: **manual** and then **high pressure**. Set cooking time to **7 minutes**.
5. After cooking cycle, do a **quick pressure release** by turning knob to **venting**.
6. Wait for steam to subside before removing lid.

7. Stir in chocolate buttons into porridge until melted. Taste. Adjust seasoning, if needed.
8. Ladle equal portions of porridge into bowls. Pour in coconut milk. Top off with chilled chocolate buttons. Serve.

Easy Mushroom Congee, Slow Cooked

Prep Time: 10 minutes; **Cook Time**: 8 hours
Recommended Serving Size: 1 cup; **Serves**: 4

Ingredients:
- 5 cups homemade/store-bought mushroom or vegetable broth/stock
- 1 cup packed fresh shiitake mushrooms, stems sliced off, caps cleaned with damp paper towels, julienned
- ½ cup white sticky rice, long-grained rinsed, drained
- ¼ cup chives, roots trimmed, minced, divided
- ¼ tsp. vegan-safe light soy sauce, add more if needed

Directions:
1. Except for chives, pour ingredients into crockpot. Stir.
2. Close lid and lock. Lid knob should be at **sealing**.
3. Press: **slow cooker**. Set cooking time to **8 hours**.
4. Wait for machine to shift to **Warm** mode. Taste. Adjust seasoning, if needed.
5. Ladle equal portions of congee into bowls. Garnish with chives before serving.

~o~

Cooking tip! Never rinse or wash fresh mushrooms or these will absorb water like a sponge. Excess moisture can make sautéing mushrooms spit out hot oil during cooking. It will add more liquid to soups and stews too, which can throw off measurements and seasonings.

To prepare fresh mushrooms, slice off and discard tougher or inedible parts (e.g. roots and stems.) Gently scrape off visible dirt using damp paper towels.

Granola Overnight Oatmeal, Slow Cooked

Prep Time: 10 minutes; **Cook Time**: 8 hours
Recommended Serving Size: ¾ cup; **Serves**: 4

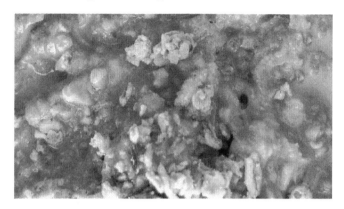

Ingredients:
- 4½ cups water
- ¾ cup steel-cut oats
- ½ cup granola or trail mix of choice, reserve half for garnish
- ¼ cup almond or cashew milk, unsweetened
- ½ Tbsp. pure maple syrup, add more if desired

Directions:
1. Except for almond milk and granola mix, pour remaining ingredients into crockpot. Stir.
2. Close lid and lock. Lid knob should be at **sealing**.
3. Press: **slow cooker**. Set cooking time to **8 hours**.
4. Wait for machine to shift to **Warm** mode.
5. Stir in half of granola mix. Taste. Adjust seasoning, if needed.
6. Ladle equal portions of oatmeal into bowls. Pour in equal amounts of almond milk. Garnish with more granola mix before serving.

~o~

Buying Tip! Always use steel cut oats or old-fashioned oats when pressure or slow cooking. Do not use instant oats or these will overcook and become paste-like.

Cooking Tip! Dried fruits also work well with this recipe. Mince the before using.

Mushroom and Barley Risotto

Prep Time: 30 to 45 minutes; **Cook Time:** 30 minutes
Recommended Serving Size: 1 cup; **Serves:** 4

Ingredients:
- 4 cups homemade/store-bought mushroom or vegetable broth/stock, unsalted
- 2/3 cup pearl barley, picked over, rinsed, drained
- 2 Tbsp. olive oil, add more if needed
- ½ pound fresh button mushrooms, roots trimmed, caps cleaned using damp paper towels, sliced into ¼-inch thick disks
- Salt and pepper to taste

Directions:
1. Press **sauté** on the **Instant Pot**. Pour oil into crockpot. Wait for oil to heat up.
2. Cooking in small batches, fry mushrooms until cooked through and browned well, but not crisp. Flip often to prevent burning. Temporarily place cooked mushrooms into a deep bowl. Repeat step for remaining mushrooms. Add more oil into crockpot only if needed. Cover bowl with saran wrap. Set aside. (See **Cooking Tip!** below.)
3. Pour barley and broth/stock into crockpot. Stir.
4. Close lid and lock. Lid knob should be at **sealing**.
5. Press: **manual** and then **high pressure**. Set cooking time to **30 minutes**.
6. After cooking cycle, do a **quick pressure release** by turning knob to **venting**.

7. Wait for steam to subside before removing lid. Turn off machine.
8. Using a whisk, stir barley so grains release more starch.
9. Stir in half of cooked mushrooms, along with most of the cooking juices that accumulated in bowl.
10. Lightly season with salt and pepper.
11. Ladle equal portions of risotto into bowls. Add cooked mushrooms on top. Serve immediately.

~O~

Cooking Tip! Fresh mushrooms are moisture-rich. To successfully cook these without having hot oil spitting constantly from the cooking surface, fry in small batches. Add only a handful of sliced mushrooms into crockpot. These will brown faster and cook more evenly, as compared to cooking ½ pound of mushrooms all at once.

To quote Ms. Julia Child, "Don't crowd the mushrooms."

After cooking these, place mushrooms in a bowl to rest. The mushrooms will release more flavorsome moisture afterwards. Stir this liquid into the risotto to amplify flavor.

For this recipe, substitute baby portabella mushrooms, if desired. Do not use canned mushrooms. These will not brown well due to its high moisture content.

Pumpkin Flavored Steel Cut Oats

Prep Time: 5 minutes; **Cook Time:** 7 minutes
Recommended Serving Size: 1 cup; **Serves:** 4

Ingredients:
- 4½ cups water
- ¾ cup steel-cut oats
- ¼ cup canned pumpkin puree
- 2 Tbsp. brown sugar, add more if desired
- 1 tsp. pumpkin spice mix

Directions:
1. Except for pumpkin spice mix, pour remaining ingredients into crockpot. Stir.
2. Close lid and lock. Lid knob should be at **sealing**.
3. Press: **manual** and then **high pressure**. Set cooking time to **7 minutes**.
4. After cooking cycle, do a **quick pressure release** by turning knob to **venting**.
5. Wait for steam to subside before removing lid. Cool slightly before proceeding.
6. Stir in pumpkin spice mix. Taste. Adjust seasoning, if needed.
7. Ladle equal portions of oats into bowls. Serve.

~o~

Instant Pot Tip! Never fill crockpot up to the brim. This will cause overflows that could damage the machine's mechanisms. This is especially true when pressure cooking. Always leave 1/3 headroom where pressure can safely build up.

It is highly recommended then to buy **Instant Pot** machines with larger capacities, e.g. 6L to 8L, even when cooking only small amount of food. A larger machine is also useful when preparing large volume of food for parties.

Teff Porridge with Fresh Bananas and Peaches, Sugar-Free

Prep Time: 15 minutes; **Cook Time**: 17 minutes
Recommended Serving Size: 1 cup; **Serves**: 4

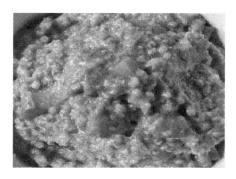

Ingredients:
- 4 cups water
- 1 cup almond or cashew milk
- ½ cup dried teff
- 2 pieces large fresh ripe peaches, peeled, pitted, cubed, reserve half for garnish
- 2 pieces large overripe bananas, peeled, mashed well

Directions:
1. Press **sauté** on the **Instant Pot**. Add in teff. Stir-fry for 5 minutes, or until grains are lightly toasted. (Do not add oil.)
2. Add in bananas and water. Stir in half of peaches.
3. Close lid and lock. Lid knob should be at **sealing**.
4. Press: **manual** and then **high pressure**. Set cooking time to **12 minutes**.
5. After cooking cycle, do a **quick pressure release** by turning knob to **venting**.
6. Wait for steam to subside before removing lid. Cool slightly before proceeding.
7. Ladle equal portions of teff porridge into bowls. Pour in almond milk. Garnish with peaches just before serving.

~o~

Buying tip! Teff is a tiny grain, approximately the size of a poppy seed. It contains high amounts of calcium, copper, iron, manganese, phosphorous, proteins, thiamine and Vitamin C, etc. It is one of the oldest known gluten-free grains in the world. It is mildly-flavored with a nutty aftertaste.

A 24-ounce bag of dried teff goes a long way. Store uncooked grains in an airtight container. This will last for more than a year, but check expiration date just to be sure.

Grain-free options

Cassava Mash

Prep Time: 10 minutes; **Cook Time**: 7 minutes
Recommended Serving Size: ½ to ¾ cup; **Serves**: 4 to 6

Ingredients:
- 2 Tbsp. brown sugar
- 2 Tbsp. Homemade Coconut Butter, divided
- 2 cups light coconut milk
- 1 cup sweetened coconut flakes, divided into four equal portions, for garnish
- 1 pound fresh cassava roots, peeled, cubed, boiled in water until fork-tender, cooled, grated; substitute frozen grated cassava if unavailable, thawed, drained well before using.

Directions:
1. Press **sauté** on the **Instant Pot**. Pour brown sugar, coconut milk, and grated cassava roots into crockpot. Add in half of coconut butter. Bring mixture to a soft simmer while stirring constantly.
2. Close lid and lock. Lid knob should be at **sealing**.
3. Press: **poultry**. Set cooking time to **5 minutes**.
4. After cooking cycle, wait for machine to shift to **Warm** mode.
5. Remove lid. Cool slightly before proceeding.
6. Using a potato masher, process cassava into fluffy mash.
7. Take 4 (4 oz. each) ramekins and line with saran wrap with generous overhangs. Spoon equal portions of mash into ramekins.
8. Place equal portions of coconut flakes into dessert plates. Carefully turn over a ramekin on coconut flakes so cassava mash sits on top. Discard saran wraps.
9. Top mash off with remaining coconut butter. Serve immediately.

Homemade Coconut Butter

Prep Time: 15 to 20 minutes depending on power of blender food processor;
No cooking required
Recommended Serving Size: 1 tsp.; **Makes multiple servings**

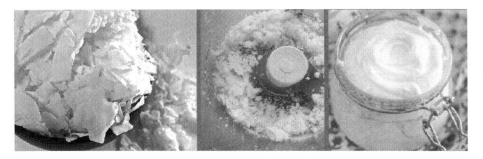

Ingredients:
- 4 cups (or more) coconut flakes

Directions:
1. Place coconut flakes into food processor or blender. Process until smooth while scraping down sides of blender jar often.
2. Place butter in airtight container. Use as needed.

Nutty Quinoa with Squash

Prep Time: 15 minutes; **Cook Time**: 16 to 20 minutes
Recommended Serving Size: 1 cup; **Serves**: 4

Ingredients:
- 2½ cups water
- 1 cup quinoa, do not rinse
- 1 pound butternut squash, peeled, deseeded, cubed
- 1 Tbsp. coconut oil
- Salt and pepper to taste

Directions:
1. Press **sauté** on the **Instant Pot**. Pour in coconut oil. Wait for oil to heat up (about 3 to 5 minutes.)
2. Add in quinoa. Stir-fry until seeds give off a nutty aroma (about 3 to 5 minutes.)
3. Stir in water and squash.
4. Close lid and lock. Lid knob should be at **sealing**.
5. Press: **manual** and then **high pressure**. Set cooking time to **10 minutes**.
6. After cooking cycle, do a **quick pressure release** by turning knob to **venting**.
7. Wait for steam to subside before removing lid.
8. Season with salt and pepper. Taste. Adjust seasoning if needed.
9. Ladle equal portions into plates. Serve while warm.

~o~

Buying tip! Quinoa is technically a seed, which makes this gluten-free. Unlike rice, different colored quinoa have same nutritional value. Buying these in bulk (e.g. 3 lb. or 4 lb. bags) is cheaper than buying several boxes in smaller portions. Store uncooked quinoa in airtight containers, away from direct sunlight. Stir-frying quinoa in oil prior to boiling releases its nut-like aroma and taste. But these can always be boiled immediately.

Potato Squeakers

Prep Time: 20 minutes; **Cook Time:** 30 to 40 minutes
Recommended Serving Size: 2 pieces; **Serves:** 4

Ingredients:
- 3 pounds Russet or Yukon Gold potatoes, skins scrubbed clean, do not peel
- 2 cups water
- ½ cup white onion, peeled, minced
- 1 Tbsp. olive oil, add more only if needed
- Salt and pepper to taste

Directions:
1. Place steaming rack/trivet into bottom of crockpot. Arrange potatoes on top.
2. Pour in water. Close lid and lock. Lid knob should be at **sealing**.
3. Press: **manual** and then **high pressure**. Set cooking time to **7 minutes**. Potatoes should be undercooked.
4. After cooking cycle, do a **quick pressure release** by turning knob to **venting**.
5. Wait for steam to subside before removing lid. Cool completely before proceeding.
6. Pour potatoes into strainer. Rinse with cool running water. Drain well.
7. Using largest blade of grater, shred potatoes, skin and all. Pat-dry with tea towel to remove excess moisture. (See **Cooking Tip!** below.)
8. Place potatoes in a bowl and mix in minced onions, salt and pepper.
10. Divide potato mix into 8 equal portions. Roll each portion into a ball, and then flatten into ½-inch thick patties. Place patties on a baking sheet lined with parchment paper.
11. Press **sauté** on the **Instant Pot**. Pour in olive oil in washed and dried crockpot. Wait for oil to heat up (about 3 to 5 minutes.)

12. Place 2 to 3 potato patties in hot oil. Fry until golden brown on one side (about 3 to 5 minutes.) Flip. Fry other side for 2 to 4 minutes. Place cooked potato squeakers on a plate lined with paper towels to drain. Repeat step for remaining patties.
13. Place 2 potato squeakers into a plate. Serve while hot either plain or with condiment of choice.

~O~

Cooking Tip! To avoid being stressed in the morning, prepare this dish well in advance. Follow recipe steps from #1 to #7. And then store shredded potatoes in a freezer-safe, re-sealable bag immediately to lessen oxidation (or browning.) Place bag in the lower part of fridge if cooking potatoes next day. If not, place bag in the freezer. Thaw and drain well before proceeding with steps #8 and after.

This dish acquired its name from the sound the potato patties make when being fried.

Cooking Tip 2! Use either all-purpose (e.g. Purple Peruvian, Yukon Gold, etc.) or starchy potatoes (e.g. Idaho Russet, Katahdin, Russet, etc.) for this recipe. These crisp up well while retaining some fluffiness when fried.

Savory Sweet Potato Mash

Prep Time: 10 minutes; **Cook Time:** 17 minutes
Recommended Serving Size: ½ to ¾ cup; **Serves:** 4 to 6

Ingredients:
- 2 Tbsp. fresh thyme, minced, reserve ¼ Tbsp. for garnish
- 1 Tbsp. homemade or store-bought coconut butter
- 1 pound orange or yellow-fleshed sweet potatoes, peeled, roughly chopped
- Water
- Salt and pepper to taste

Directions:
1. Place sweet potatoes into crockpot. Cover with water.
2. Close lid and lock. Lid knob should be at **sealing**.
3. Press: **manual** and then **high pressure**. Set cooking time to **12 minutes**.
4. After cooking cycle, do a **quick pressure release** by turning knob to **venting**.
5. Wait for steam to subside before removing lid. Cool slightly before proceeding.
6. Carefully pour out sweet potatoes into strainer. Discard cooking liquid. Return sweet potatoes into same (unwashed) crockpot.
7. Press **sauté** on the **Instant Pot**.
8. Pour coconut butter and minced thyme into crockpot.
9. Using potato masher, process sweet potatoes to desired consistency (either chunky or smooth.) Turn off machine.
10. Season with salt and pepper.
11. Ladle equal portions into small dessert bowls. Garnish with remaining thyme just before serving.

Sweet Hominy with Coconut Flakes

Prep Time: 20 minutes including soaking time; **Cook Time**: 50 minutes
Recommended Serving Size: ¾ cup; **Serves**: 4 to 6

Ingredients:
- 3 cups water
- 1 cup freshly grated coconut meat, substitute sweetened coconut flakes, for garnish, optional
- 1 Tbsp. white sugar, add more if needed
- 1 12 oz. pack dried white hominy or pozole kernels, picked over, soaked in water for 15 minutes, rinsed, drained well
- 1 can 15 oz. thick coconut cream

Directions:
1. Pour hominy, sugar, and water into crockpot. Stir.
2. Close lid and lock. Lid knob should be at **sealing**.
3. Press: **manual** and then **high pressure**. Set cooking time to **50 minutes**. Corn kernels should be fully "bloomed" or doubled/tripled in size.
4. After cooking cycle, do a **quick pressure release** by turning knob to **venting**.
5. Wait for steam to subside before removing lid.
6. Stir in coconut cream. Taste. Adjust seasoning if needed.
7. Ladle equal portions into bowls. Garnish with grated coconut meat, if using. Cool slightly before serving.

~o~

Cooking Tip! Dried hominy or pozole corn is cheaper than canned ones, but the latter is easier to use because these are already cooked. Rinse and drain these well before using. Cut cooking time to only 10 minutes when pressure cooking canned hominy.

This ingredient benefits from prolonged cooking. Use this in slow cooked soups and stews.

Vanilla Quinoa with Almond Meal

Prep Time: 15 minutes; **Cook Time**: 12 minutes
Recommended Serving Size: 1 cup; **Serves**: 4

Ingredients:
- 2½ cups almond milk, add more if desired
- 1 cup quinoa, rinsed, drained
- ½ cup almond meal
- 1 Tbsp. white sugar
- 1 piece tiny/small vanilla bean, halved lengthwise, insides scraped

Directions:
1. Pour ingredients (including vanilla pod and scrapings) into crockpot. Stir.
2. Close lid and lock. Lid knob should be at **sealing**.
3. Press: **manual** and then **high pressure**. Set cooking time to **12 minutes**.
4. After cooking cycle, do a **quick pressure release** by turning knob to **venting**.
5. Wait for steam to subside before removing lid.
6. Fish out and discard vanilla pod. Taste. Adjust seasoning if needed.
7. Ladle equal portions into plates. Pour in more almond milk, if desired. Cool slightly before serving.

~o~

Cooking tip! Adding almond meal makes this dish light, while providing a pleasant mouth-feel. If unavailable, use any coarsely ground nuts, preferably unsalted.

Cooking Tip 2! Whenever possible, use vanilla beans (a.k.a. vanilla pods and vanilla sticks) to season sweet dishes. These are more fragrant and strongly flavored than vanilla essences/extracts. One tiny or small bean is enough for most recipes serving between 4 and 20 people.

If using the vanilla essences/extracts, always add these to dishes **when heat is off**. These are alcohol-based, which means that their aroma and taste will evaporate in high heat. Use only recommended amount indicated per recipe. Using too much will overpower the taste of dishes.

Chapter 3. Easy and Quick Lunch Selections

Salads and Sandwiches

Breadless Pizza with Squash Flower Toppings

Prep Time: 20 minutes; **Cook Time:** 7 to 10 minutes
Recommended Serving Size: ¼ pizza; **Serves:** 4

Ingredients:
- 2 Tbsp. extra virgin olive oil, divided
- 1 Tbsp. Vegan-Safe Extremely Garlicky Basil Pesto, add more if needed
- 1 pound squash blossoms, sepals and stems removed, rinsed, drained, pat-dried using paper towels to remove excess moisture
- ½ cup store-bought vegan mozzarella cheese, freshly grated, divided
- ⅛ cup **Homemade Vegan Parmesan Cheese**, reserve 1 tsp. for pizza base
-

Directions:
1. Line bottom of crockpot with sheets of parchment paper with generous overhangs.
2. Sprinkle in half of **Homemade Vegan Parmesan Cheese**, then layer mozzarella cheese on top.
3. Dot surface of pizza base with **Vegan-Safe Extremely Garlicky Basil Pesto**.

4. Arrange squash blossoms on top. Drizzle in olive oil. Finally, top off pizza with remaining parmesan cheese.
5. Press **sauté** on the **Instant Pot**. Seal lid but do not lock. Cook pizza for 7 to 10 minutes, or until cheese is completely melted, and edges of pizza base are lightly brown. Do not flip over.
6. Remove lid. Turn off machine immediately.
7. Carefully extract pizza from crockpot by gently tugging at the paper overhangs. Place on wooden chopping board. Slice pizza into eights or quarters.
8. Serve with more Homemade **Vegan Extremely Garlicky Basil Pesto** on the side if desired.

Vegan-Safe Extremely Garlicky Basil Pesto

Prep Time: 3 to 5 minutes depending on power of blender food processor;
No cooking required
Recommended Serving Size: 1 Tbsp.; **Makes multiple servings**

Ingredients:
- 2 cups packed, fresh basil leaves, rinsed, drained well
- ½ cup cashew or pine nuts, freshly toasted on dry pan, cooled completely to room temperature before using
- ¼ cup garlic cloves, peeled, roughly chopped
- ½ cup extra virgin olive oil
- Salt and pepper to taste

Directions:
1. Except for salt and pepper, pour remaining ingredients into food processor or blender. Process until smooth while scraping down sides of blender jar often.
2. Stir in salt and pepper. Taste. Adjust seasoning if needed.
3. Place butter in airtight container. Use as needed.

Homemade Vegan Parmesan Cheese

Prep Time: 5 to 10 minutes depending on power of blender food processor;
No cooking required
Recommended Serving Size: 1 Tbsp.; **Makes multiple servings**

Ingredients:
- 6 Tbsp. nutritional yeast
- 1½ cups raw cashew nuts
- 1 tsp. level kosher salt, add more if needed
- ½ tsp. garlic or onion powder

Directions:
1. Except for salt, pour remaining ingredients into food processor or blender. Process until well combined.
2. Stir in salt. Taste. Adjust seasoning if needed.
3. Place cheese in airtight container. Use as needed.

Horta (Steamed Spinach with Lemon Juice)

Prep Time: 5 minutes; **Cook Time**: 10 minutes
Recommended Serving Size: 1 cup; **Serves**: 4 to 6

Ingredients:
- 3 pounds fresh spinach leaves, picked over, rinsed, squeeze-dried (See **Cooking Tip!** below)
- 2 Tbsp. extra virgin olive oil, add more if needed
- 1 piece large lemon, ½ juiced, remaining ½ sliced into wedges
- 1 cup water
- Salt and pepper to taste

Directions:
1. Place spinach into steaming basket. Pour water into base of crockpot and set filled steaming basket on top.
2. Close lid and lock. Lid knob should be at **sealing**.
3. Press: **steam**.
4. Wait for machine to shift to **Warm** mode. Turn off machine. Remove lid. Cool slightly before proceeding.
5. Remove steaming basket from crockpot. Drain spinach well.
6. Pour spinach into large mixing bowl. Using a fork, gently loosen leaves while stirring in lemon juice and olive oil.
7. Serve equal portions into plates with wedges of lemon on the side. Season with salt and pepper just before eating.

~0~

Cooking Tip! *Horta* (roughly translated as "wild mountain greens) is a traditional Greek dish with multiple variations, depending on the region. Essentially, this is a dish made from steaming greens and adding generous amounts of extra virgin olive oil and lemon juice as seasoning.

One of the best things about this dish is that it can be served right out of the steamer, or at room temperature, or even chilled.

Other variations of this dish are:

- Amaranth greens
- Beetroot greens/tops
- Broccoli rabe a.k.a. *rapini*
- Carrot tops
- Chicory greens
- Collard greens
- Curly endives
- Dandelion greens and/or flowers
- Fennel leaves
- *Gai Lan* or Chinese broccoli, which is similar in appearance and taste to broccoli rabe
- Kale
- *Kangkong* or Chinese swamp cabbage
- Nettles
- Poppy leaves
- Purslane leaves
- Swiss chard
- Turnip greens
- Watercress
- Wild sorrel
- Wild spinach

Some recipes call for the addition of other ingredients like: boiled potatoes, brined capers, fresh Kalamata olives, minced chilis, roasted nuts, toasted garlic, etc. Use any herb(s) or add vegan cheese if desired.

In smaller portions, *horta* can also be used as an appetizer or side dish.

Lemon and Soy Portobello Mushrooms

Prep Time: 35 minutes including marinating time; **Cook Time**: 15 minutes
Recommended Serving Size: 1 cup; **Serves**: 4

Ingredients:
- 8 pieces large fresh Portobello or shiitake mushrooms caps, stems removed, cleaned well using damp paper towels
- 4 pieces large sourdough rolls (or any vegan-safe bun,) halved horizontally, cut-sides lightly toasted
- 2 Tbsp. freshly squeezed lemon juice
- 2 Tbsp. *tamari* or light soy sauce
- 2 Tbsp. olive oil, divided, add more if needed

Directions:
1. Season mushrooms with lemon juice, soy sauce, and half of olive oil. Chill in fridge for at least 30 minutes before frying. Drain well but reserve marinade.
2. Press **sauté**. Pour remaining oil into crockpot. Wait for oil to heat up (about 3 to 5 minutes.)
3. Cooking in batches, fry mushrooms until browned on both sides. Flip mushrooms often to prevent burning. Temporarily place partially cooked mushrooms on a holding plate. Repeat step for remaining mushrooms. Add more oil into crockpot only if needed.
4. Return mushrooms into crockpot, along with remaining marinade.
5. Close lid and lock. Lid knob should be at **sealing**.
6. Press: **poultry**. Set cooking time to **5 minutes**.
7. Wait for machine to shift to **Warm** mode. Remove lid. Cool slightly before proceeding.
8. Place two mushrooms into sourdough rolls, along with some of the cooking juices. Serve plain or with fresh salad on the side. Serve immediately.

Millet and Zucchini Salad

Prep Time: 10 minutes; **Cook Time:** 17 minutes
Recommended Serving Size: 1 cup; **Serves:** 4

Ingredients:
- 2 Tbsp. homemade or store-bought vegan-safe pesto, add more if needed
- 1 Tbsp. extra virgin olive oil, add more only if needed
- 2 cups water
- 1¼ cups millet, rinsed, drained
- 1 cup zucchini, skin scrubbed clean, do not peel, sliced into ¼-inch thick half-moons, drained well, pat-dried using paper towels

Directions:
1. Press **sauté** on the Instant Pot. Pour oil into crockpot. Wait for oil to heat up.
2. Cooking in batches, fry zucchini chips until lightly seared on both sides. Flip often to prevent burning. Temporarily place partially cooked vegetables on a holding plate. Repeat step for remaining zucchini chips. Add more oil into crockpot only if needed. Set aside.
3. Pour millet and water into same (unwashed) crockpot. Stir.
4. Close lid and lock. Lid knob should be at **sealing**.
5. Press: **manual** and then **high pressure**. Set cooking time to **12 minutes**.
6. After cooking cycle, do a **quick pressure release** by turning knob to **venting**.
7. Wait for steam to subside before removing lid. Turn off machine.
8. Using a fork, fluff up millet while stirring in pesto and cooked zucchini (including cooking juices.) Taste. Adjust seasoning if needed.
9. Ladle equal portions into salad bowls. Serve.

Spicy Mushroom and Rice Burrito Filling

Prep Time: 35 minutes; **Cook Time**: 10 minutes
Recommended Serving Size: ½ burrito; **Serves**: 4

Ingredients:
- 4 cups **Basic Tomato Rice**
- ¼ cup vegan sharp cheddar cheese, grated, divided
- 1 piece large fresh jalapeno or serrano pepper, stemmed, minced
- 1 can 15 oz. black beans in water, rinsed, drained
- 1 can 15 oz. button mushrooms, pieces and stems, rinsed, drained

Also:
- 2 pieces 12-inch (or larger) wheat tortillas, heated through
- 1 cup water

Directions:
1. Place black beans, **Basic Tomato Rice**, minced jalapeno pepper, and mushrooms into steamer-safe bowl.[5] Stir. Seal with aluminum foil.
2. Place steaming rack/trivet into bottom of crockpot. Place bowl on top. Pour in water.
3. Close lid and lock. Lid knob should be at **sealing**.
4. Press: **steam**.
5. Wait for machine to shift to **Warm** mode. Remove lid. Cool slightly before proceeding.
6. Carefully remove bowl from crockpot. Stir cheese into rice mixture.
7. Place equal portions of rice mixture into both tortillas. Form into thick, long logs. Fold one end of tortilla over, and tuck in the sides. Roll burrito tightly.
8. Just before serving, equally halve burritos.

---

[5] Steamer-safe bowl should easily fit inside the crockpot.

Warm Potato Salad

Prep Time: 10 minutes; **Cook Time:** 15 minutes not including depressurization
Recommended Serving Size: ¼ cup; **Serves:** 4

Ingredients:
- 2 pounds marble potatoes, skins scrubbed clean, do not peel, halved
- 1 piece small shallots, peeled, julienned
- ¼ Tbsp. kosher salt, add more if needed
- ⅛ cup loosely packed fresh parsley, roughly torn
- Water

Directions:
1. Combine salt and shallots in a small bowl. Mash well so that shallots releases moisture. Set aside.
2. Place potatoes into crockpot. Cover with water.
3. Close lid and lock. Lid knob should be at **sealing**.
4. Press: **manual** and then **high pressure**. Set cooking time to **15 minutes**.
5. After cooking cycle, opt for **natural pressure release**. This could take between **15 and 20 minutes**.
6. Wait for machine to shift to **Warm** mode.
7. Carefully pour out potatoes into strainer. Discard cooking liquid. Drain well.
8. To assemble: place cooked potatoes, parsley, and shallots (including liquids) into a bowl. Toss to combine. Set aside for 10 minutes to steep.
9. Serve at room temperature in small portions. Or, reheat in microwave oven for 5 seconds at highest temperature.

Tomato Rice Dishes

Basic Tomato Rice

Prep Time: 5 minutes; **Cook Time:** 18 to 25 minutes
Recommended Serving Size: 1 cup; **Serves:** 4

Ingredients:
- 4½ cups water
- 2 cups white rice, rinsed until water runs clear, drained
- 1 piece large very ripe tomato, skin scrubbed clean, bottom scored
- 1 Tbsp. extra virgin olive oil
- Salt and pepper to taste

Directions:
1. Pour olive oil, rice, and water into crockpot. Gently stir. Place whole tomato bottom-side up in the middle.
2. Close lid and lock. Lid knob should be at **sealing**.
3. Press: **rice cooker**.
4. Wait for machine to shift to **Warm** mode. Remove lid.
5. Using a rice paddle, break up tomato while fluffing up rice. Season with salt and pepper. Taste. Adjust seasoning if needed.
6. Ladle equal portions into plates. Serve.

~o~

Cooking tip! Some **Instant Pot** models come with their own measuring cups. Use these when cooking rice. If accessory is not available, use any measuring cup at hand. Just make sure to use same tool to measure both rice and water.

Black Beans, Corn, Tomato in Brown Rice

Prep Time: 10 minutes; **Cook Time:** 22 minutes
Recommended Serving Size: 1 cup; **Serves:** 4

Ingredients:
- 4½ cups water
- 1½ cups brown rice, rinsed until water runs clear, drained
- 1 cup canned whole corn kernels, drained well
- 1 cup very ripe tomato, deseeded, minced
- 1 Tbsp. canned salted black beans, rinsed, drained

Directions:
1. Pour ingredients into crockpot. Gently stir.
2. Close lid and lock. Lid knob should be at **sealing**.
3. Press: **manual** and then **high pressure**. Set cooking time to **22 minutes**.
4. After cooking cycle, opt for **quick pressure release** by turning knob to **venting**.
5. Wait for steam to subside before removing lid.
6. Using a rice paddle, fluff up rice.
7. Ladle equal portions of rice into plates. Serve.

~o~

Buying tip! Salted black beans (sometimes labeled fermented black beans) are available in Asian section of most grocery stores. These come in tiny cans and are extremely salty. Use sparingly. If unavailable, substitute canned, unseasoned black beans, but season rice with salt.

Black Olives in Tomato Rice

Prep Time: 10 minutes; **Cook Time:** 18 to 25 minutes
Recommended Serving Size: 1 cup; **Serves:** 4

Ingredients:
- 4½ cups water
- 2 cups Basmati rice, rinsed until water runs clear, drained
- 1 cup very ripe tomato, deseeded, minced
- ¼ cup black olives in brine, pitted, lightly drained, sliced into ¼-inch thick rings
- ¼ tsp. vegan-safe balsamic vinegar, optional

Directions:
1. Pour ingredients into crockpot. Gently stir.
2. Close lid and lock. Lid knob should be at **sealing**.
3. Press: **rice cooker**.
4. Wait for machine to shift to **Warm** mode. Remove lid.
5. Using a rice paddle, fluff up rice.
6. Ladle equal portions into plates. Serve.

~0~

Cooking Tip! Substitute brined capers for black olives, if desired. Substitute unsalted mushroom or vegetable broth/stock for water. For a more fragrant dish, garnish with fresh cilantro just before serving. This recipe also works well with light sprinkling of lemon juice, instead of balsamic vinegar.

Black Rice with Green Onions

Prep Time: 10 minutes; **Cook Time:** 25 minutes
Recommended Serving Size: 1 cup; **Serves:** 6 to 8

Ingredients:
- 4½ cups Homemade Vegetable Stock
- 2 cups black rice or wild rice, rinsed until water runs clear, drained
- ½ cup tomato or spaghetti sauce
- ¼ cup vegan cheddar cheese, diced
- ⅛ cup green onions, roots trimmed, minced

Directions:
1. Except for cheddar cheese and green onions, pour ingredients into crockpot. Gently stir.
2. Close lid and lock. Lid knob should be at **sealing**.
3. Press: **manual** and then **high pressure**. Set cooking time to **22 minutes**.
4. After cooking cycle, opt for **quick pressure release** by turning knob to **venting**.
5. Wait for steam to subside before removing lid.
6. Using a rice paddle, fluff up rice.
7. Ladle equal portions of rice into plates. Garnish with green onions and vegan cheese just before using.

~O~

Cooking Tip! As a variation, remove cheddar cheese from this recipe. Substitute with 1 Tbsp. good quality extra virgin oil, 1 tsp. fresh bird's eye chili (minced,) and ¼ tsp. kosher salt. Cooked shelled edamame beans and/or green peas also work well in this recipe.

Homemade Mushroom Stock

Prep Time: 15 minutes; **Cook Time**: 20 minutes
Makes multiple servings

Ingredients:
- 8 cups water
- 1 pound button mushrooms, inedible parts sliced off, cleaned well using damp paper towels, thinly sliced
- ¼ pound dried shiitake mushrooms, inedible parts sliced off
- ⅛ pound leeks, roots trimmed, minced
- Salt and pepper to taste, optional

Also
- Kitchen scraps: any vegetables past their prime, mushrooms trimmings, etc.

Directions:
1. Except for salt and pepper, pour remaining ingredients into crockpot. Stir.
2. Press: **manual** and then **high pressure**. Set cooking time to **20 minutes**.
3. After cooking cycle, opt for **quick pressure release** by turning knob to **venting**.
4. Wait for steam to subside before removing lid. Cool completely to room temperature before proceeding.
5. Strain out and discard solids.
6. Season stock with salt and pepper, if using. Taste. Adjust seasoning if needed.

~0~

Cooking Tip! To make this dish versatile, it is best to leave out the salt and pepper for later. This allows you to control the amount of seasonings when using stock for other dishes. Use any edible combination of fresh and dried mushrooms for maximum flavor. Store stock in airtight containers in the fridge. These can also be frozen in single portions, or approximately: 1 cup.

Homemade Vegetable Stock

Prep Time: 20 minutes; **Cook Time:** 27 to 30 minutes
Makes multiple servings

Ingredients:
- 8 cups water
- 4 cups mirepoix (See **Cooking Tip!** below)
- 2 Tbsp. fresh garlic, peeled, minced
- 2 Tbsp. olive oil
- Salt and pepper to taste, optional

Also
- Kitchen scraps: any vegetables past their prime, mushrooms trimmings, etc.

Directions:
1. Press **sauté** on the **Instant Pot**. Pour in oil and mirepoix.
2. Cook vegetables down until soft and transparent (7 to 10 minutes.)
3. Except for salt and pepper, pour remaining ingredients into crockpot. Stir.
4. Press: **manual** and then **high pressure**. Set cooking time to **20 minutes**.
5. After cooking cycle, opt for **quick pressure release** by turning knob to **venting**.
6. Wait for steam to subside before removing lid. Cool completely to room temperature before proceeding.
7. Strain out and discard solids.
8. Season stock with salt and pepper, if using. Use as needed.

~0~

Cooking Tip! Technically, **mirepoix** refers to the process of cooking vegetables in low heat until these caramelize without browning too much. However, this can also refer to the vegetables commonly used during cooking. In this case: **mirepoix** refers to: 2 cups onions or shallots (peeled, diced), 1 cup carrots (unpeeled, tops removed, diced,) and 1 cup celery (roots trimmed, strings removed, chopped.)

Other variations of **mirepoix** to try are:

- *Dexulles* (French) – herbs, onions/shallots, and mushrooms
- *Ginisa* (Filipino) – garlic, onions/shallots, and tomatoes
- *Mirepoix* (Cajun and American) – bell peppers, celery, and onions/shallots
- *Refogado* (Portuguese) – garlic, onions, and tomatoes
- *Soffritto* (Italian) – carrots, celery, garlic, onions/shallots, and parsley
- *Suppengrun* (German) – carrots, celeriac, and leeks
- *Wloszczyzna* (Polish) – bell peppers, carrots, celeriac, and onions

Chickpea and Tomato Rice

Prep Time: 10 minutes; **Cook Time:** 18 to 25 minutes
Recommended Serving Size: 1 cup; **Serves:** 4

Ingredients:
- 4½ cups water
- 2 cups white rice, rinsed until water runs clear, drained
- 1 cup very ripe tomato, deseeded, minced
- ½ cup canned chickpeas in water, rinsed, drained well
- Salt and pepper to taste

Directions:
1. Except for salt and pepper, pour remaining ingredients into crockpot. Gently stir.
2. Close lid and lock. Lid knob should be at **sealing**.
3. Press: **rice cooker**.
4. Wait for machine to shift to **Warm** mode. Remove lid.
5. Using a rice paddle, fluff up rice. Season with salt and pepper as you go. Taste. Adjust seasoning if needed.
6. Ladle equal portions into plates. Serve immediately.

~o~

Cooking Tip! If canned chickpeas are not available, substitute equal amounts of canned: Great Norther beans, kidney beans, or lima beans – or use a combination of. Canned or frozen corn kernels also work well for this recipe, as well as fresh squash (peeled, deseeded, cubed.) For a more fragrant dish, garnish with minced chives, cilantro, or parsley just before serving. For a bit of heat, add desired amount of minced fresh chili, like: jalapeno or serrano pepper.

One Pot Java Rice

Prep Time: 10 minutes; **Cook Time:** 18 to 25 minutes
Recommended Serving Size: 1 cup; **Serves:** 4

Ingredients:
- 4½ cups water
- 2 cups brown rice, rinsed until water runs clear, drained
- 3 Tbsp. tomato catsup
- ½ Tbsp. brown sugar
- ⅛ Tbsp. kosher salt, add more if needed

Directions:
1. Except for catsup and salt, pour remaining ingredients into crockpot. Gently stir.
2. Close lid and lock. Lid knob should be at **sealing**.
3. Press: **manual** and then **high pressure**. Set cooking time to **22 minutes**.
4. After cooking cycle, opt for **quick pressure release** by turning knob to **venting**.
5. Wait for steam to subside before removing lid.
6. Using a rice paddle, fluff up rice while stirring in catsup and salt. Taste. Adjust seasoning if needed.
7. Ladle equal portions of rice into plates. Serve immediately.

~o~

Cooking Tip! To make this dish more substantial, add ½ cup frozen vegetables (e.g. green peas, carrots, corn, or a combination of, no need to thaw) to the rice just before cooking. Or, add canned whole button or shiitake mushrooms (preferably with tiny caps) to the rice just before fluffing this up, just to heat through.

Chapter 4. Family Dinners and Main Courses

Risotto and pasta dishes

Barley and Beetroot Risotto

Prep Time: 20 minutes; **Cook Time:** 37 to 42 minutes
Recommended Serving Size: 1 cup; **Serves:** 4 to 6

Ingredients:
- 6 cups Homemade Vegetable Stock
- 2 cups pearl barley, picked over, rinsed, drained
- ½ cup green onions, roots trimmed, reserved half for garnish
- 3 pieces large beetroots, peeled, cubed (See **Cooking Tip!** below)
- 2 Tbsp. extra virgin olive oil, add more if needed

Directions:
1. Press **sauté** on the **Instant Pot**. Pour in olive oil. Wait for oil to heat up (about 3 to 5 minutes.)
2. Cooking in small batches, fry beetroots until lightly seared on all sides. Add more oil into crockpot only when needed. Temporarily place partially cooked beetroots into bowl (about 7 to 10 minutes.)
3. Stir-fry half of green onions in remaining oil until softened (about 2 minutes.)
4. Except for beetroots and garnish, stir in remaining ingredients into crockpot.
5. Close lid and lock. Lid knob should be at **sealing**.

6. Press: **manual** and then **high pressure**. Set cooking time to **18 minutes**.
7. After cooking cycle, opt for **quick pressure release** by turning knob to **venting**.
8. Wait for steam to subside before removing lid.
9. Press **sauté** once more.
10. Whisk barley pearls so that these will release more starch.
11. Stir in partially cooked beetroots and all the cooking juices. Put lid on but do not lock. Cook risotto for another 5 minutes or until beetroots are fork-tender. Stir occasionally to prevent risotto from burning.
12. Ladle equal portions of barley into plates. Garnish with remaining green onions just before serving.

~O~

Cooking Tip! Beetroots taste wonderful and lend dishes an incredibly vibrant color. But these stain hands, chopping boards and plastic containers. It is highly recommended to wear food-safe gloves when handling beetroots. To prevent staining plastic or wooden chopping boards, wrap these in saran wrap before using. Use only glass containers or metal-based cooking implements like: ladles or spatulas. Serve dish and store leftovers in ceramic or glass containers.

Easy Barley and Mushroom Risotto

Prep Time: 10 minutes; **Cook Time:** 26 to 30 minutes
Recommended Serving Size: 1 cup; **Serves:** 4

Ingredients:
- 4½ cups Homemade Mushroom Stock
- 1 pound fresh shiitake mushrooms, stems removed, caps cleaned well using damp paper towels, julienned
- 1 cup pearl barley, picked over, rinsed, drained
- 1 Tbsp. extra virgin olive oil, add more if needed
- ¼ tsp. kosher salt, add more if needed

Directions:
1. Press **sauté** on the **Instant Pot**. Pour in olive oil. Wait for oil to heat up (about 3 to 5 minutes.)
2. Add in half of mushrooms. Stir-fry until mushrooms brown and release some of their moisture (about 5 to 7 minutes.) Transfer partially cooked mushrooms into a holding plate. Repeat step for all mushrooms. Pour in more olive oil into crockpot, only if needed. Return mushrooms to crockpot, including cooking juices.
3. Except for kosher salt, stir in remaining ingredients.
4. Close lid and lock. Lid knob should be at **sealing.**
5. Press: **manual** and then **high pressure.** Set cooking time to **18 minutes.**
6. After cooking cycle, opt for **quick pressure release** by turning knob to **venting.**
7. Wait for steam to subside before removing lid.
8. Whisk barley pearls so that these will release more starch. Season with salt. Taste. Adjust seasoning if needed.
9. Ladle equal portions into plates. Serve.

Lemony Asparagus Risotto

Prep Time: 10 minutes; **Cook Time:** 17 minutes
Recommended Serving Size: 1 cup; **Serves:** 4

Ingredients:
- 4½ cups homemade/store-bought mushroom or vegetable broth/stock
- 1½ pounds thick-stemmed asparagus, tough ends snapped off, 2-inch tops sliced off and set aside; remaining stems minced
- 1 cup pearl barley, picked over, rinsed, drained
- ½ piece small lemon, freshly juiced
- ⅛ tsp. kosher salt, add more if needed

Directions:
1. Pour pearl barley and Homemade Vegetable Stock, along with chopped asparagus stems. Stir.
2. Close lid and lock. Lid knob should be at **sealing.**
3. Press: **manual** and then **high pressure**. Set cooking time to **18 minutes.**
4. After cooking cycle, opt for **quick pressure release** by turning knob to **venting.**
5. Wait for steam to subside before removing lid.
6. Press **sauté** on the **Instant Pot**. Whisk barley pearls so these will release more starch. Stir in asparagus tops. Cook only for 2 minutes, or until asparagus tops turn one shade brighter.
7. Season with salt. Taste. Adjust seasoning if needed.
8. Ladle equal portions into plates. Serve.

Milk and Macaroni Soup

Prep Time: 10 minutes; **Cook Time:** 5 to 7 minutes
Recommended Serving Size: 1 cup; **Serves:** 4

Ingredients:
- 3 cups Homemade Vegetable Stock
- 1 cup almond milk
- 1 cup elbow macaroni, uncooked
- 1 cup frozen vegetable mix, preferably with minced carrots, corn and peas, thawed, drained well
- ¼ cup celery stalks, strings removed, minced

Directions:
1. Except for almond milk, pour remaining ingredients into crockpot.
2. Close lid and lock. Lid knob should be at **sealing**.
3. Press: **manual** and then **high pressure**. Set cooking time to **3 minutes**.
4. After cooking cycle, opt for **quick pressure release** by turning knob to **venting**.
5. Wait for steam to subside before removing lid.
6. Press **sauté** on the **Instant Pot**. Cook until macaroni is cooked to desired firmness.[6]
7. Stir in almond milk. Turn off machine.
8. Ladle equal portions into bowls. Serve immediately.

---

[6] For this recipe, macaroni should be slightly overcook. Add toasted fresh chives, garlic flakes, or toasted onion strings for garnish if desired.

Mushroom Stroganoff, Slow Cooked

Prep Time: 10 minutes; **Cook Time:** 13 to 17 minutes
Recommended Serving Size: 1 cup; **Serves:** 4

Ingredients:
- 3 cups Homemade Mushroom Stock
- 1 can 15 oz. thick coconut cream
- 2 Tbsp. olive oil, add more if needed
- 1 pound fresh white mushrooms, stems removed, caps cleaned well using damp paper towels, sliced into ¼-inch thick disks
- Salt and pepper to taste

Directions:
1. Press **sauté** on the **Instant Pot**. Pour in olive oil. Wait for oil to heat up (about 3 to 5 minutes.)
2. Add in half of mushrooms. Stir-fry until mushrooms brown a little and release some of their moisture (about 5 to 7 minutes.) Transfer partially cooked mushrooms into a holding plate. Repeat step for all mushrooms. Pour in more olive oil into crockpot, only if needed. Return mushrooms to crockpot, including cooking juices.
3. Stir in broth/stock.
4. Close lid and lock. Lid knob should be at **sealing**.
5. Press: **poultry**. Set cooking time to **5 minutes**.
6. Wait for machine to shift to **Warm** mode. Turn off machine.
7. Stir in coconut cream. Season with salt and pepper.
8. Serve this on cooked pasta, freshly steamed rice, or toasted bread. This can also be used as filling, e.g.
9. **Baozi (Steamed Buns) Filled with Mushroom** Stroganoff.

Pumpkin in Tagliatelle

Prep Time: 15 minutes not including pasta cooking time; **Cook Time**: 15 minutes
Recommended Serving Size: 1 cup; **Serves**: 4

Ingredients:
- 3 cups vegan-safe tagliatelle, cooked al dente according to package instructions, reserve 1 cup of its cooking liquid
- 2 cups Homemade Vegetable Stock
- ½ cup loosely packed vegan mozzarella chesses, shredded
- 2 Tbsp. homemade or store-bought basil pesto, add more if needed
- 1 pound pumpkin, peeled, deseeded, cubed

Directions:
1. Pour Homemade Vegetable Stock into crockpot, along with pumpkin cubes.
2. Close lid and lock. Lid knob should be at **sealing**.
3. Press: **manual** and then **high pressure**. Set cooking time to **12 minutes**.
4. After cooking cycle, opt for **quick pressure release** by turning knob to **venting**.
5. Wait for steam to subside before removing lid.
6. Press **sauté** on the **Instant Pot**.
7. Gently stir in cheese, pesto, and tagliatelle until cheese melts. If sauce seems too dry, pour in pasta cooking water a little bit at a time until desired consistency is achieved. Taste. Adjust seasoning if needed.
8. Ladle equal portions into plates. Serve immediately.

~0~

Cooking tip! This recipe also works well with carrots, squash, and even purple taro – or a combination of. Use parsley or walnut pesto, if desired. Use other long pasta, if desired (e.g. *bigoli, bucatini, capellini, fusilli bucati*, or plain spaghetti.)

Soups and Stews

Butternut Squash Soup with Almonds

Prep Time: 20 minutes including toasting time; **Cook Time**: 12 minutes
Recommended Serving Size: ¾ cup; **Serves**: 4 to 6

Ingredients:
- 4 cups Homemade Vegetable Stock
- 1 piece medium butternut squash, peeled, deseeded, roughly chopped
- ½ cup almond slivers, toasted on a dry pan
- ½ cup leeks, roots trimmed, minced
- Salt and white pepper to taste

Directions:
1. Except for salt and pepper, pour remaining ingredients into crockpot. Stir.
2. Close lid and lock. Lid knob should be at **sealing**.
3. Press: **manual** and then **high pressure**. Set cooking time to **12 minutes**.
4. After cooking cycle, do a **quick pressure release** by turning knob to **venting**.
5. Wait for steam to subside before removing lid.
6. Using an immersion blender, process soup to desired consistency (e.g. chunky or smooth.)
7. Season lightly with salt and pepper.
8. Ladle equal portions into bowls. Cool slightly before serving. Serve plain or with vegan-safe bread or croutons.

~0~

Cooking Tip! This recipe also works well with carrots, frozen green peas (no need to thaw,) parsnips, and pumpkins. Use chopped cashew nuts or pined nuts, if desired.

Chunky Lentil and Tomato Soup

Prep Time: 10 minutes; **Cook Time:** 25 minutes
Recommended Serving Size: 1 cup; **Serves:** 4

Ingredients:
- 3 cups Homemade Vegetable Stock
- 1 can 15 oz. whole tomatoes
- ½ cup dried French or green lentils, picked over, rinsed, drained
- ⅛ cup fresh parsley, minced, for garnish
- Salt and pepper to taste

Directions:
1. Pour Homemade Vegetable Stock and lentils into crockpot. Stir.
2. Close lid and lock. Lid knob should be at **sealing**.
3. Press: **manual** and then **high pressure**. Set cooking time to **20 minutes**.
4. After cooking cycle, do a **quick pressure release** by turning knob to **venting**.
5. Wait for steam to subside before removing lid.
6. Press **sauté**. Stir in whole tomatoes. Break into smaller chunks. Cook only for 5 minutes or until tomatoes are heated through.
7. Season with salt and pepper. Taste. Adjust seasoning if needed.
8. Ladle equal portions into bowls. Garnish with parsley just before serving.

Easy Miso Soup with Tteokbokki

Prep Time: 10 minutes; **Cook Time:** 4 minutes
Recommended Serving Size: 1 cup; **Serves:** 4

Ingredients:
- 4 Tbsp. vegan-safe red miso paste
- 4 cups homemade or store-bought mushroom broth/stock
- 1 cup *tteokbokki* or cylindrical rice cakes
- ½ cup green onions, roots trimmed, minced
- 1 tsp. light soy sauce, add more if needed

Optional
- ½ cup canned shiitake mushrooms, rinsed, drained
- ½ cup fresh napa cabbage, rinsed, drained, julienned

Directions:
1. Pour mushrooms broth/stock, light soy sauce and *tteokbokki* into crockpot. Stir.
2. Close lid and lock. Lid knob should be at **sealing**.
3. Press: **manual** and then **high pressure**. Set cooking time to **3 minutes**.
4. After cooking cycle, do a **quick pressure release** by turning knob to **venting**.
5. Wait for steam to subside before removing lid.
6. Press **sauté**. Dissolve miso paste into soup. Stir in optional ingredients, if using.
7. Turn off machine. Taste. Adjust seasoning if needed.
8. Ladle equal portions into bowls. Garnish with green onions just before serving.

~0~

Buying Tip! *Tteokbokki* or rice cakes are available in the Asian section of some grocery stores, and in shops that sell Korean food and condiments. These are usually sold in different shapes and sizes. Some are sold in blocks (like tofu blocks.) Do not overcook *tteokbokki* or these will dissolve completely in the soup. Some people prefer chewier *tteokbokki*, in which case, shorten pressure cooking time by a minute.

Mushrooms in Vermicelli Noodle Soup

Prep Time: 20 minutes including soaking time; **Cook Time**: 50 minutes
Recommended Serving Size: 1¼ cups; **Serves**: 4 to 6

Ingredients:
- 8 oz. vermicelli noodles (a.k.a. bean thread noodles,) soaked in warm water for 15 minutes, lightly drained, discard soaking liquid
- 8 cups Homemade Vegetable Stock
- ½ cup green onions, roots trimmed, minced, reserved half for garnish
- 1 can 15 oz. shiitake mushrooms, julienned
- ½ tsp. tamari or light soy sauce, add more if needed

Directions:
1. Except for garnish, pour ingredients into crockpot. Stir.
2. Close lid but do not lock. Press: **poultry.**
3. Wait for machine to shift to **Warm** mode. Remove lid. Cool slightly before proceeding. Turn off machine.
4. Taste. Adjust seasoning if needed.
5. Ladle equal portions into bowls. Just before serving, garnish with remaining green onions.

Spiced Hominy Stew

Prep Time: 20 minutes including soaking time; **Cook Time**: 50 minutes
Recommended Serving Size: ¾ cup; **Serves**: 4 to 6

Ingredients:
- 4 cups Homemade Vegetable Stock
- 1 can 15 oz. diced zesty chili style tomatoes, or diced tomatoes with green chilies
- 1 12 oz. pack dried white hominy or pozole kernels, picked over, soaked in water for 15 minutes, rinsed, drained well
- 1 cup frozen mixed veggies, thawed
- Salt and pepper to taste

Directions:
1. Pour hominy and Homemade Vegetable Stock into crockpot. Stir.
2. Close lid and lock. Lid knob should be at **sealing**.
3. Press: **manual** and then **high pressure**. Set cooking time to **50 minutes**. Corn kernels should be fully "bloomed" or doubled in size.
4. After cooking cycle, do a **quick pressure release** by turning knob to **venting**.
5. Wait for steam to subside before removing lid. Press **sauté** on the **Instant Pot**.
6. Stir in remaining ingredients. Bring stew to a soft simmer (about 10 minutes) to heat vegetables through. Turn off machine. Taste. Adjust seasoning if needed.
7. Ladle equal portions into bowls. Cool slightly before serving.

~o~

Cooking tip! This recipe is versatile. Use any combination of fresh or frozen vegetables for this recipe. Add dried or fresh chilies, if desired. If hominy is unavailable, substitute dried chickpeas or white beans.

White Beans and Kale Stew

Prep Time: 20 minutes; **Cook Time:** 50 minutes
Recommended Serving Size: 1 cup; **Serves:** 4 to 6

Ingredients:
- 4 cups Homemade Mushroom Stock
- 2 Tbsp. *herbes de provence*, or any spice blend of choice
- 1 pound fresh kale, leaf ribs and stems removed, leaves julienned, rinsed, drained
- ¼ pound dried Great Northern beans or lima beans, picked over, rinsed, drained
- Salt and pepper to taste

Directions:
1. Pour Homemade Mushroom Stock and white beans into crockpot. Stir.
2. Close lid and lock. Lid knob should be at **sealing**.
3. Press: **manual** and then **high pressure**. Set cooking time to **30 minutes**.
4. After cooking cycle, do a **quick pressure release** by turning knob to **venting**.
5. Wait for steam to subside before removing lid.
6. Stir in remaining ingredients. Taste. Adjust seasoning if needed. Turn off machine.
7. Ladle equal portions into bowls. Cool slightly before serving.

~O~

Cooking Tip! For hectic days, substitute 1 15 oz. can of beans of choice. Reduce cooking time by **3 minutes**. Substitute baby spinach leaves for kale. For a bit of heat, add 1 piece bird's eye chili to the stew prior to pressure cooking.

Chapter 5. Desserts and Sweets

Filling desserts

Creamy Sweet Potato Mash

Prep Time: 10 minutes; **Cook Time:** 17 minutes
Recommended Serving Size: ¼ cup; **Serves:** 4 to 6

Ingredients:
- 2 cans 15 oz. thick coconut cream
- 2 Tbsp. white sugar
- 2 tsp. homemade or store-bought coconut butter, add more if desired
- 1 pound white-fleshed sweet potatoes, peeled, roughly chopped
- Water

Directions:
1. Place sweet potatoes into crockpot. Cover with water.
2. Close lid and lock. Lid knob should be at **sealing**.
3. Press: **manual** and then **high pressure**. Set cooking time to **12 minutes**.
4. After cooking cycle, do a **quick pressure release** by turning knob to **venting**.
5. Wait for steam to subside before removing lid. Cool slightly before proceeding.
6. Carefully pour out sweet potatoes into strainer. Discard cooking liquid. Return sweet potatoes into same (unwashed) crockpot.
7. Press **sauté** on the **Instant Pot**.

8. Pour remaining ingredients into crockpot.
9. Using potato masher, process sweet potatoes to desired consistency (either chunky or smooth.) Turn off machine.
10. Ladle equal portions into small dessert bowls. Serve.

Palitaw (Rice Ball Patties with Coconut Flakes and Sesame Seeds)

Prep Time: 20 minutes; **Cook Time:** 10 to 20 minutes
Recommended Serving Size: 2 pieces; **Serves:** 4

Ingredients:
- 3½ cups water, divided
- 1 cup glutinous rice flour
- ½ cup brown sugar
- 2 Tbsp. sesame seeds, toasted well on a dry pan
- 2 pounds freshly grated coconut meat or coconut flakes

Directions:
1. Pour 2 cups of water into crockpot. Press **sauté**. Put lid on but do not seal. Wait for water to come to a rolling boil.
2. Meanwhile, combine ½ cup of water with rice flour in a bowl. Stir until dough comes together. Divide into 8 equal portions. With clean, dry hands, roll individual portions into balls. Flatten to inch-thick patties.
3. Place rice ball patties on baking sheet lined with parchment paper. Cover with sheet of saran wrap to rest.
4. In another bowl, combine brown sugar, grated coconut and toasted sesame seeds. Divide into two equal portions and place into two separate containers, one as garnish, the other for coating.
5. When water boils, carefully and gently drop 4 pieces of rice ball patties into water. These are cooked as soon as these rise to the surface (approx. 2 minutes.) Using slotted spoon, remove patties from hot water and place on colander to drain. Do not stack on top of each other or these will stick. After lightly draining, roll each patty into coconut flakes-sesame seed mixture until generously coated. Place on a serving plate. Repeat step for remaining rice ball patties.
6. Place two rice ball patties into plates. Garnish with desired amount of coconut flakes-sesame seed mixture. Serve.

Stewed Apples with Walnuts

Prep Time: 20 minutes; **Cook Time:** 10 minutes
Recommended Serving Size: 1 piece; **Serves:** 4 to 6, depending on size of cooker

Ingredients:
- 4 to 6 pieces medium apples, preferably Cortland, Fuji, or Granny Smith, skins scrubbed clean, pat-dried using paper towels, stemmed, cored
- 1 cup water
- ½ cup brown sugar
- ½ cup raisins or sultanas
- ¼ cup store-bought roasted walnuts, lightly salted, roughly chopped

Directions:
1. Combine raisins, sugar and walnuts into a small bowl. Divide into 4 or 6 equal portions. Stuff these (as best as you can) into apple cavities. Reserve leftovers.
2. Place stuffed apples into crockpot. Pour in water and leftover stuffing.
3. Close lid and lock. Lid knob should be at **sealing.**
4. Press: **manual** and then **high pressure.** Set cooking time to **10 minutes.**
5. After cooking cycle, do a **quick pressure release** by turning knob to **venting.**
6. Wait for steam to subside before removing lid. Cool slightly before proceeding.
7. Ladle apples into dessert bowls. Pour small amount of stewing liquid over apples. Serve warm.

-0-

Cooking Tip! Substitute pears for the apples. Substitute cashew nuts or pecans for the walnuts. To add more sweetness to the dish, substitute other dried fruits (e.g. cranberries, dates, or prunes) for the raisins.

Sweet Chickpeas in Almond Milk (No Pre-Soaking)

Prep Time: 5 minutes; **Cook Time:** 55 minutes
Recommended Serving Size: ½ cup; **Serves:** 4 to 6

Ingredients:
- 8 cups water, divided
- 2 cups brown sugar
- 1 cup chilled almond milk, divided, for serving
- 1 pound dried chickpeas/garbanzos, picked over, rinsed, drained

Directions:
1. Pour 7 cups of water and chickpeas into crockpot.
2. Close lid and lock. Lid knob should be at **sealing**.
3. Press: **manual** and then **high pressure**. Set cooking time to **40 minutes**.
4. After cooking cycle, do a **quick pressure release** by turning knob to **venting**.
5. Wait for steam to subside before removing lid. Cool slightly before proceeding.
6. Pour chickpeas and water into colander. Rinse. Drain well.
7. Return chickpeas into (unwashed) crockpot. Stir in brown sugar and remaining water.
8. Press **sauté**. Bring water to a rolling boil. Cook chickpeas until water is reduced by a quarter. Turn off machine. Cool chickpeas more before using.
9. Ladle equal portions into dessert bowls. Pour small amount of almond milk into dessert bowls just before serving.

Taho (Silken Tofu with Tapioca Pearls)

Prep Time: 20 minutes; **Cook Time**: 8 minutes, not including depressurization
Recommended Serving Size: 1 cup; **Serves**: 4

Ingredients:
- 3 cups water
- ¾ cup brown sugar
- ½ cup dried tapioca pearls, any size, picked over, rinsed, drained
- 1 12 oz. block soft silken tofu, placed in cheesecloth-lined colander, drained well, sliced into 4 equal portions, chilled

Directions:
1. Except for silken tofu, pour remaining ingredients into crockpot. Stir.
2. Close lid and lock. Lid knob should be at **sealing**.
3. Press: **manual** and then **high pressure**. Set cooking time to **8 minutes**.
4. After cooking cycle, opt for **natural pressure release**. This could take between 15 and 20 minutes. Cool slightly before proceeding.
5. Remove lid. Stir contents of crockpot to prevent tapioca pearls from sticking to each other. Cool further before using.
6. Ladle equal portions of chilled silken tofu into dessert bowls. Spoon over tapioca pearls and syrup on top. Serve immediately.

Ube Halaya (Purple Yam Mash)

Prep Time: 10 minutes; **Cook Time**: 17 minutes
Recommended Serving Size: ½ cup; **Serves**: 6 to 8

Ingredients:
- 2½ pounds purple yam, skins scrubbed clean, do not peel
- 2 cans 15 oz. thick coconut cream
- ½ cup homemade/store-bought coconut butter, add more for shinier surface
- ¼ cup brown sugar
- Water

Directions:
1. Place purple yams into crockpot. Cover with water.
2. Close lid and lock. Lid knob should be at **sealing**.
3. Press: **manual** and then **high pressure**. Set cooking time to **15 minutes**.
4. After cooking cycle, do a **quick pressure release** by turning knob to **venting**.
5. Wait for steam to subside before removing lid. Cool completely to room temperature before proceeding.
6. Pour out yams into strainer. Discard cooking liquid. Rinse out crockpot.
7. Peel yams by hand. Using largest blade of grater, shred yams.
8. Press **sauté** on the **Instant Pot**.
9. Return yams into crockpot, and pour in remaining ingredients.
10. Using potato masher, process taro into smooth paste. Add more coconut butter to make yam look shinier, if desired. Mix well after each addition. Turn off machine.
11. Ladle equal portions into 4 (4-ounce each) ramekins lined with saran wrap with generous overhangs. Seal ramekins with saran wrap. Chill in fridge for 30 minutes or until set.
12. Turn ramekin over into small dessert plate. Serve.

Short and sweet (cooks in 20 minutes or less)

Boiled Plantains

Prep Time: 5 minutes; **Cook Time:** 10 minutes
Recommended Serving Size: 2 pieces; **Serves:** 4

  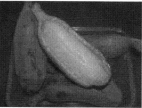

Ingredients:
- 8 pieces medium overripe *cardaba* or *saba* plantians, stems trimmed, skins scrubbed clean, do not peel
- Water

Directions:
1. Place plantains whole into crockpot. Cover with water.
2. Close lid and lock. Lid knob should be at **sealing**.
3. Press: **manual** and then **high pressure**. Set cooking time to **10 minutes**.
4. After cooking cycle, do a **quick pressure release** by turning knob to **venting**.
5. Wait for steam to subside before removing lid. Cool slightly before proceeding.
6. Pour out plantains into strainer. Discard cooking liquid.
7. Place two pieces of plantains per dessert plate. Serve warm. Peel boiled plantains before eating.

~o~

Buying Tip! *Cardana* or *saba* are some of the smallest plantain cultivars in the world. These are sold green and unripe in most grocery stores. Let these ripen at home. For this recipe, using overripe and mushy plantains is highly recommended. These become sweeter when boiled.

Bubur Cha Cha (Root Crops Stewed in Coconut Cream)

Prep Time: 20 minutes; **Cook Time**: 10 minutes
Recommended Serving Size: 2 pieces; **Serves**: 4 to 6

Ingredients:
- 2 cans 15 oz. thick coconut cream
- 2 cups *cardaba* or *saba* ripe plantains, peeled, sliced into inch thick disks
- 1 cup purple yam, peeled, cubed (approx. same size as plantain disks)
- 1 cup sweet potato, peeled, cubed (approx. same size as plantain disks)
- ½ cup brown sugar, add more if desired

Directions:
1. Place ingredients into crockpot.
2. Close lid and lock. Lid knob should be at **sealing**.
3. Press: **manual** and then **high pressure**. Set cooking time to **12 minutes**.
4. After cooking cycle, do a **quick pressure release** by turning knob to **venting**.
5. Wait for steam to subside before removing lid. Cool slightly before proceeding.
6. Taste. Adjust seasoning if needed.
7. Ladle equal portions into bowls. Cool slightly before serving.

Chocolate Raspberry Pudding with Chia Seeds

Prep Time: 20 minutes; **Cook Time:** 5 minutes
Recommended Serving Size: 1 piece; **Serves:** 4

Ingredients:
- 2 Tbsp. brown sugar
- 1½ cups almond milk
- ½ cup chia seeds
- ¼ cup vegan-safe dark chocolate buttons/chips
- 1 to ½ cup fresh raspberries, stemmed, chilled well before using

Directions:
1. Pour almond milk and brown sugar into crockpot.
2. Close lid and lock. Lid knob should be at **sealing**.
3. Press: **poultry**. Set timer to **5 minutes**.
4. Wait for machine to shift to **Warm** mode. Turn off machine. Carefully remove lid. Cool completely to room temperature before proceeding.
5. Except for raspberries, stir in remaining ingredients until chocolate melts. Seal lid. Set aside for 10 minutes or until chia seeds have absorbed all the liquids.
6. Spoon equal portions into dessert cups or bowls. Chill in fridge for at least two hours before serving. Top off with raspberries just before serving.

~o~

Cooking Tip! There are many possible variations to this dish. Other than almond milk, use: cashew nut milk, hazelnut milk, oat milk, quinoa milk, rice milk, soy milk, and thin coconut milk. Fresh apricots, bananas, cherries, cranberries, dates, dragon fruits, figs, honeydew, pears, pineapples, and strawberries work wonderfully well with dark chocolate too. Flax seeds have stronger flavor, but can be used instead of chia seeds.

Kluai Buad Chi (Almond Milk Stewed Bananas)

Prep Time: 10 minutes; **Cook Time:** 5 minutes
Recommended Serving Size: 1 cup; **Serves:** 4 to 6

Ingredients:
- 4 to 6 pieces medium almost ripe bananas, quartered or sliced into thirds
- 2 cups almond milk
- ¼ cup brown sugar, add more if desired
- 1 Tbsp. corn flour
- 1/16 tsp. vanilla extract

Directions:
1. Pour almond milk and corn flour into crockpot. Stir until latter dissolves.
2. Add in brown sugar and bananas.
3. Close lid and lock. Lid knob should be at **sealing**.
4. Press: **poultry**. Set timer to **5 minutes**.
5. Wait for machine to shift to **Warm** mode. Turn off machine. Carefully remove lid.
6. Stir in vanilla extract.
7. Ladle equal portions into small dessert bowls. Serve.

Orange-Scented Tapioca Pearls

Prep Time: 20 minutes; **Cook Time:** 8 minutes, not including depressurization
Recommended Serving Size: 1 cup; **Serves:** 4

Ingredients:
- 4 cups almond milk
- ½ cup dried tapioca pearls, tiny/small, picked over, rinsed, drained
- ¼ cup white sugar, add more if needed
- 1 piece tiny/small vanilla bean, halved lengthwise, insides scraped, reserve half bean for garnish
- 1 piece small orange, zest removed using vegetable peeler, pulp reserved for other dishes

Also
- 1 piece tiny/small sprig of mint, for garnish, optional

Directions:
1. Except for garnishes, pour remaining ingredients into crockpot. Stir.
2. Close lid and lock. Lid knob should be at **sealing**.
3. Press: **manual** and then **high pressure**. Set cooking time to **8 minutes**.
4. After cooking cycle, opt for **natural pressure release**. This could take between 15 and 20 minutes. Cool slightly before proceeding.
5. Remove lid. Stir contents of crockpot to prevent tapioca pearls from sticking to each other. Cool further before using.
6. Fish out and discard spent vanilla bean half and orange zests.
7. Taste. Adjust seasoning if needed.
8. Ladle cooked tapioca into large serving bowl. Garnish with mint and remaining vanilla pod. Ladle equal portions into bowls.

Steamed Peanut Butter Cups

Prep Time: 20 minutes; **Cook Time:** 10 to 20 minutes
Recommended Serving Size: 1 piece; **Serves:** 4

Ingredients:
- 2 cups water
- 1½ cups vegan safe dark chocolate buttons or chips, divided into 8 equal portions
- ¼ cup smooth peanut butter, divided into 4 equal portions

Directions:
1. Place steaming rack/trivet into bottom of crockpot. Pour in water.
2. Place paper liners into 4 steamer-safe ramekins.
3. Place a portion of chocolate buttons each into prepared ramekins. Add in a portion of peanut butter. Top off with another portion of chocolate buttons. Repeat step for remaining ingredients.
4. Seal ramekins with aluminum foil. Arrange ramekins on top of steaming rack.
5. Close lid and lock. Lid knob should be at **sealing**.
6. Press: **steam**.
7. Wait for machine to shift to **Warm** mode. Turn off machine. Remove lid. Cool completely to room temperature before proceeding.
8. Remove ramekins from steaming basket and set on countertop to cool further. Chill in fridge for at least two hours.
9. Remove peanut butter cups from ramekins. Serve immediately.

Chapter 6. Bread and Savory Snacks

Easy bread recipes

Baozi (Steamed Buns) Filled with Mushroom Stroganoff

Prep Time: 3 to 3½ hours, including proofing bread; **Cook Time**: 15 to 45 minutes
Recommended Serving Size: 1 piece; **Serves**: 8

Ingredients:
Bread
- 5 cups all-purpose flour, sifted twice, add more for kneading
- 2 cups warm water
- ½ cup white sugar
- 2¼ tsp. dry instant yeast (1 packet)
- 1 ¼ Tbsp. baking powder

Also
- 6 Tbsp. coconut oil, melted
- 2 cups water for steaming

Filling
- 1¼ cups **Mushroom Stroganoff, Slow Cooked**, lightly drained, divided into 8 portions

Directions:
1. Combine sugar, water, and yeast in a bowl. Set aside for 15 minutes or until mixture becomes foamy.
2. Stir in remaining bread ingredients. Mix until dough comes together.
3. On a lightly floured surface, turn out dough. Knead until no longer sticky.

4. Place dough in a large bowl. Add in coconut oil. Turn dough until well-coated. Cover bowl with saran wrap. Set aside for 1½ hours, or until dough doubles.
5. Punch dough down. Turn out dough again on flat surface. (Oil should prevent this from sticking.) Knead until elastic.
6. Divide into 8 equal portions. Roll each portion into balls, tucking in seams underneath.
7. Using a rolling pin, flatten each ball into 6-inch wide disks. Edges should be thinner than the centers.
8. To assemble: spoon one portion of **Mushroom Stroganoff**, Slow Cooked into center of each dough.
9. Pull and pinch in edges to completely cover filling. Twist to seal.
10. Place buns, twist sides down, on small sheets of wax paper to prevent these from sticking to steaming basket.
11. Place 2 filled buns into bamboo steaming baskets. There should be ample space for dough to expand in.
12. Place steaming rack into bottom of crockpot. Pour in 2 cups of water.
13. Place filled bamboo steaming baskets on top.
14. Close lid and lock. Lid knob should be at **sealing**.
15. Press: **steam**. Set cooking time to **15 minutes**.
16. After cooking cycle, remove lid. Cool slightly before removing steaming baskets, and then the *baozi*. Repeat step for filled buns.
17. Place *baozi* on serving plate to cool slightly. Serve. Remove wax paper only before eating.

~O~

Cooking Tip! *Bao* or *pao* (steamed buns) has no filling, and is often served with soups and stews. To make: use the same recipe as indicated above, but skip steps #7 to #9. If desired, fillings can be added later. Do not overcook, or bread will turn brown.

Crockpot Bread Loaf, Slow Cooked

Prep Time: 3 to 3½ hours; **Cook Time**: 2½ to 4 hours
Recommended Serving Size: 1 thick slice or 2 thinner slices; **Makes**: 1 loaf

Ingredients:
- 6½ cups all-purpose flour, divided
- 3 cups lukewarm water
- 1 Tbsp. sugar
- 1 Tbsp. heaping instant dry yeast
- 1 Tbsp. kosher salt

Directions:
1. Combine sugar, water, and yeast in a large bowl. Set aside for 15 minutes or until mixture becomes foamy.
2. Stir in 5½ cups of flour and salt. Mix until dough comes together.
3. On a lightly floured surface, turn out dough. Knead until no longer sticky. Add more flour as needed.
4. Return dough to the same (used) bowl. Cover with saran wrap. Set aside for 1½ hours, or until dough doubles in size.
5. Punch dough down. Turn dough out again on lightly floured surface. Knead until smooth.
6. Roll dough into large ball, tucking in seams underneath.
7. Line crockpot with sheets of parchment paper with generous overhangs. Place dough into crockpot. Let dough proof for another hour.
8. Close lid and lock. Lid knob should be at **sealing**.
9. Press **slow cook** on the **Instant Pot**. Set to **highest temperature** and at **2½ hours**. Test for doneness by inserting a skewer in center of bread. If dough is still wet, continue cooking for another 1 to 1½ hours. Test for doneness in 30 minute intervals. When skewer comes out clean, turn off machine immediately.
10. Carefully remove bread from crockpot by tugging on the paper parchment overhangs.
11. Place bread on a rack to cool to room temperature before slicing. Use as needed.

~0~

Cooking Tip! Crockpot bread is usually light colored. This will never have bronzed or crusty tops. Overcooking this in the **Instant Pot** will only scorch the bottom, and make the bread denser. It also doesn't help to flip the bread over to cook the other side. This will only remove most of the air within.

If desired, place cooled crockpot bread under the broiler to brown the top, or slice the bread and toast these individually instead.

Spread small amount of **Homemade Coconut Butter** on toasted bread slices as a quick snack option.

Easy No-Bake Flatbread

Prep Time: 3 to 3½ hours; **Cook Time:** 18 to 30 minutes
Recommended Serving Size: 1 piece; **Serves:** 6

Ingredients:
- 2½ cups unbleached all-purpose flour, add more for kneading
- ¾ cup warm water
- 2¼ tsp. dry instant yeast (1 packet)
- ¾ tsp. kosher salt
- ½ tsp. white sugar

Also
- 3 Tbsp. olive oil

Directions:
1. Combine sugar, water, and yeast in a bowl. Set aside for 15 minutes or until mixture becomes foamy.
2. Stir in flour and salt. Mix until dough comes together.
3. On a lightly floured surface, turn out dough. Knead until no longer sticky.
4. Place dough in a large bowl. Pour in oil. Turn dough until well-coated. Cover bowl with saran wrap. Set aside for 1½ hours, or until dough doubles in size.
5. Punch dough down. Turn out dough again. (Oil should prevent this from sticking to the surface.) Knead until elastic. Divide into 6 equal portions.
6. Roll each portion into balls, tucking in seams underneath.
7. Using a rolling pin, flatten each ball into ¼-inch thin disks. Place rolled dough on sheets of parchment paper. Set aside for at least another 30 minutes to proof.
8. Press **sauté** on the **Instant Pot**. Wait for crockpot to heat up (3 to 5 minutes.)
9. Place one flatbread into crockpot. Dry fry until air pockets form and brown in spots (3 to 5 minutes.) Edges should be firm and not doughy to the touch. Flip. Do same for other side. Place cooked flatbread in between tea towels to keep warm. Repeat step for remaining flatbreads.
10. Serve warm plain, or with vegan cheese, or with condiments of choice (e.g. chili sauce.)

Garlic Beer Pita Bread

Prep Time: 3 to 3½ hours; **Cook Time**: 18 to 30 minutes
Recommended Serving Size: 1 piece; **Serves**: 6

Ingredients:
- 2½ cups all-purpose flour, add more for kneading
- 1 cup beer, heated in microwave oven until lukewarm
- 2¼ tsp. dry instant yeast (1 packet)
- 1 tsp. kosher salt
- ½ tsp. garlic powder

Also
- 3 Tbsp. olive oil

Directions:
1. Except for oil, combine ingredients in a bowl. Mix until dough comes together.
2. On a lightly floured surface, turn out dough. Knead until no longer sticky.
3. Place dough in a large bowl. Pour in oil. Turn dough until well-coated. Cover bowl with saran wrap. Set aside for an hour, or until dough doubles in size.
4. Punch dough down. Turn out dough again. (Oil should prevent this from sticking to the surface.) Knead until elastic. Divide into 6 equal portions.
5. Roll each portion into balls, tucking in seams underneath.
6. Using a rolling pin, flatten each ball into ¼-inch thin disks. Place rolled dough on sheets of parchment paper. Set aside for at least another 30 minutes to proof.
7. Press **sauté** on the **Instant Pot**. Wait for crockpot to heat up (3 to 5 minutes.)
8. Place one flatbread into crockpot. Dry fry until air pockets form and brown in spots (3 to 5 minutes.) Do not pop air pockets! Edges should be firm and not doughy to the touch. Flip. Do the same for other side. Place cooked flatbread in between tea towels to keep warm. Repeat step for remaining flatbreads.
9. Serve warm plain, or with vegan cheese.

Putong Bigas (Steamed Rice Cakes)

Prep Time: 20 minutes, not including soaking time; **Cook Time**: 30 to 45 minutes
Recommended Serving Size: 2 pieces; **Serves**: 6 to 8

Ingredients:
- 4 cups rice flour, sifted
- 2 cups water, plus 1 cup more for steaming
- 1½ cups white sugar
- 3 Tbsp. baking powder
- 1 can 15 oz. thick coconut cream

Also
- Coconut oil for greasing

Directions:
1. Pour 2 cups of water into a bowl. Stir in coconut cream and rice flour. Cover bowl with saran wrap. Refrigerate for at least 12 hours before using.
2. Stir in baking powder and sugar. Set aside until mixture comes to room temperature.
3. Using a pastry brush, lightly grease 10 to 12 pieces of ramekins (3 oz. each) with oil. Pour in batter until 2/3 full.
4. Place steaming rack/trivet into bottom of crockpot. Pour in remaining water.
5. Cooking in batches, place 3 or 4 filled ramekins on top of steaming rack. Close lid and lock. Lid knob should be at **sealing**. Press: **steam**. Set cooking time to **15 minutes**. After cooking cycle, remove lid. Cool slightly before removing ramekins. Repeat step for remaining ingredients.
6. Place cooked cakes on rack to cool. Loosen edges of cakes from ramekins using a butter knife. Place rice cakes on small plates. Serve while warm.

Ube Puto (Steamed Purple Yam Cakes)

Prep Time: 10 minutes; **Cook Time:** 40 to 45 minutes
Recommended Serving Size: 3 to 4 pieces; **Serves:** 4 to 6

Ingredients:
- 1½ Tbsp. baking powder
- 1¾ cup coconut milk
- 1 cup all-purpose flour
- ½ cup purple yam powder
- ½ cup white sugar

Also
- Banana leaves, rinsed, drained, softened over open flame, torn into thick strips
- 1 cup water

Directions:
1. Line 12 (3" each) silicon cups with banana leaves with generous overhangs.
2. Sift baking powder, flour, and sugar twice. Place into a bowl.
3. Stir in coconut milk. Mix until ingredients are well incorporated.
4. Pour batter into prepared silicon cups until 2/3 full.
5. Place steaming rack/trivet into bottom of crockpot. Pour in water.
6. Cooking in batches, place 5 to 6 filled silicon cups on top of steaming rack. Close lid and lock. Lid knob should be at **sealing**. Press: **steam**. Set cooking time to **15 to 20 minutes**. After cooking cycle, remove lid. Cool slightly before removing silicon cups. Repeat step for remaining ingredients.
7. Place cooked cakes on rack to cool. Pry cakes from silicon cups by gently tugging on banana leaves. Place rice cakes on small plates. Serve while warm.

Vegetable-based

Aloo Pakora (Potato Fritters)

Prep Time: 10 minutes; **Cook Time:** 19 to 21 minutes
Recommended Serving Size: ½ cup loosely packed; **Serves:** 4

Ingredients:
- 4 Tbsp. coconut oil, add more if needed
- 4 Tbsp. corn flour, add more if needed
- 2 cups potatoes, preferably Russet or Yukon Gold, peeled, diced, rinsed, drained well, pat-dried using paper towels to remove excess moisture
- 2 cups water
- Salt and pepper to taste

Directions:
1. Place potatoes into crockpot. Pour in water.
2. Close lid and lock. Lid knob should be at **sealing**.
3. Press: **manual** and then **high pressure**. Set cooking time to **4 minutes**. Potatoes should be undercooked.
4. After cooking cycle, do a **quick pressure release** by turning knob to **venting**.
5. Wait for steam to subside before removing lid. Cool completely before proceeding.
6. Pour potatoes into strainer. Rinse with cool running water. Drain.
7. Rinse out and dry crockpot.
8. Place potatoes in a bowl and mix in corn flour, salt and pepper.
9. Press **sauté** on the **Instant Pot**. Pour coconut oil into crockpot. Wait for oil to heat up (about 3 to 5 minutes.)
10. Drop heaping tablespoons of potato mix into hot oil. Fry for **7 to 10 minutes** until golden brown on all sides. Place cooked fritters

on a plate lined with paper towels to drain. Repeat step for remaining potatoes.
11. Place 3 or 4 fritters into a plate. Serve while hot.

Boiled Edamame in Pods

Prep Time: 2 minutes; **Cook Time:** 1 minute
Recommended Serving Size: 1 cup; **Serves:** 4 to 6

Ingredients:
- 1½ pounds fresh edamame in pods, rinsed, drained, do not use shelled edamame
- ¼ cup kosher salt
- Water

Directions:
1. Place edamame and salt into crockpot. Submerge pods under two inches of water.
2. Close lid and lock. Lid knob should be at **sealing**.
3. Press: **manual** and then **high pressure**. Set cooking time to **1 minute**.
4. After cooking cycle, do a **quick pressure release** by turning knob to **venting**.
5. Wait for steam to subside before removing lid. Cool slightly before proceeding.
6. Pour edamame pods into colander. Rinse to remove excess salt. Drain well.
7. Cool completely to room temperature before serving. Extract beans from pods when eating. Discard pods.

Boiled Peanuts

Prep Time: 5 to 15 minutes, depending on how clean unshelled peanuts are;
Cook Time: 30 to 45 minutes
Recommended Serving Size: 1 cup; **Serves:** 4 to 6

Ingredients:
- 2½ pounds raw unshelled peanuts, picked over, shells scrubbed clean of visible dirt, drained
- 2/3 cup kosher salt
- Water

Directions:
1. Place peanuts and salt into crockpot. Submerge peanuts under 2 inches of water.
2. Close lid and lock. Lid knob should be at **sealing**.
3. Press: **manual** and then **high pressure**. Set cooking time to **30 minutes** for firm peanuts or **45 minutes** for mushy peanuts. (See **Cooking Tip!** below.)
4. After cooking cycle, do a **quick pressure release** by turning knob to **venting**.
5. Wait for steam to subside before removing lid. Cool slightly before proceeding.
6. Pour peanuts into colander. Rinse to remove excess salt. Drain well.
7. Cool peanuts to room temperature before serving in small bags.

~0~

Cooking Tip! Boiled peanuts are best when a little mushy. This makes them easier to eat. Some people prefer something chewier though. Adjust cooking time depending on personal taste. Always boil unshelled peanuts with plenty of water and salt.

Corn on the Cob with Coconut Butter

Prep Time: 5 minutes; **Cook Time:** 3 minutes
Recommended Serving Size: 1 corn cob; **Serves:** 4

Ingredients:
- 4 large ears of fresh sweet corns, preferably Aces, Cabo or Japanese cultivars, husked, silks removed, rinsed, drained
- 2 cups water
- 2 tsp. Homemade Coconut Butter
- 1 tsp. kosher salt

Directions:
1. Place steaming rack/trivet into bottom of crockpot. Arrange corn cobs on top. If pieces are too large, halve these.
2. Pour in water. Close lid and lock. Lid knob should be at **sealing**.
3. Press: **manual** and then **high pressure**. Set cooking time to **3 minutes**.
4. After cooking cycle, do a **quick pressure release** by turning knob to **venting**.
5. Wait for steam to subside before removing lid. Cool slightly before proceeding.
6. Place corn cob on individual plates. Using a pastry brush, spread Homemade Coconut Butter evenly all over corn. Season lightly with salt. Serve.

~0~

Buying Tip! Fresh corn kernels look plump and tightly packed. Not-so-fresh ones look desiccated, dimpled, and widely spaced apart. Although these are still edible, these are better suited for dishes with high liquid content, e.g. soups and stews.

Corn *Pakora* (Sweet Corn Fritters)

Prep Time: 10 minutes; **Cook Time:** 19 to 21 minutes
Recommended Serving Size: 1 fritter; **Serves:** 4

Ingredients:
- 2 Tbsp. coconut oil, add more if needed
- 2 cans 15 oz. each whole corn kernels, rinsed, drained lightly
- 2 tsp. corn flour
- ½ tsp. *chalat* or *garam* masala, or any spice blend of choice
- Salt and pepper to taste

Directions:
1. Press **sauté** on the **Instant Pot**. Pour in oil. Wait for oil to heat up.
2. Meanwhile, combine remaining ingredients in a bowl. Divide into 4 equal portions. Shape portions into patties.
3. Carefully place 2 patties into hot oil. Fry for **8 minutes**, or until brown on both sides. Flip patties often but carefully to prevent these from breaking apart. Place on plates lined with paper towels to drain. Repeat step for remaining patties. Add more oil into crockpot only if needed.
4. Serve fritters while hot with favorite condiment, e.g. hot sauce or Flavored Vinegar.

Flavored Vinegar

Pinakurat

Prep Time: 15 minutes; **No cooking required**
Recommended Serving Size: 1 to 2 tsp.; **Makes multiple servings**

Ingredients:
- 2 Tbsp. heaping black peppercorns
- 1½ cups coconut vinegar
- ¼ pound bird's eye chili, stemmed, rinsed, drained well, for more heat, mince half
- 1 piece large shallot, peeled, minced
- 1 piece medium garlic head, cloves peeled, thinly sliced

Directions:
1. Pour ingredients into non-reactive container with tight-fitting lid.
2. Let ingredients steep for at least 3 hours at room temperature.
3. Shake bottle well before using. Use as needed.

Sinamak

Prep Time: 5 minutes; **No cooking required**
Recommended Serving Size: 1 to 2 tsp.; **Makes multiple servings**

Ingredients:
- 1½ cups coconut vinegar
- 1 cup bird's eye chili, stemmed, rinsed, drained well, mince 4 to 5 pieces
- 1 piece thumb-sized ginger, peeled, sliced into ¼-inch thick strips
- 1 piece large white onion, peeled, sliced into ¼-inch thick strips
- 1 piece medium garlic head, cloves peeled, whole

Directions:
1. Pour ingredients into non-reactive container with tight-fitting lid.
2. Let ingredients steep for at least 3 hours at room temperature.
3. Shake bottle well before using. Use as needed.

Salty and Sweet Chickpeas

Prep Time: 5 minutes; **Cook Time:** 20 minutes
Recommended Serving Size: ½ cup; **Serves:** 4 to 6

Ingredients:
- 3 cups vinegar
- ¼ cup brown sugar
- 2 cans 15 oz. chickpeas, rinsed, drained well
- 1 tsp. extra virgin olive oil
- ¼ tsp. kosher salt, add more if needed

Directions:
1. Pour chickpeas and vinegar into crockpot. Close lid and lock. Lid knob should be at **sealing**.
2. Press: **poultry**.
3. Wait for machine to shift to **Warm** mode. Remove lid. Cool slightly before proceeding.
4. Pour chickpeas into strainer. Drain well. Do not rinse. Return chickpeas into crockpot.
5. Press **sauté** on the **Instant Pot**.
6. Pour in remaining ingredients. Stirring often, cook until sugar dissolves. Turn off machine immediately.
7. Carefully pour seasoned chickpeas into small heat-resistant bowls. Cool to room temperature before serving.

~0~

Instant Pot Tip! Sticky dishes like the one above can make scrubbing out the crockpot a pain. The best way to remove the sugar residue is to pour in water until crockpot is 2/3 full. Close lid and lock. Press either **Meat/Stew** or **Soup**. Wait for machine to shift to **Warm** mode. Remove lid. Cool slightly before proceeding.

Place crockpot into the sink. Add a few drops of dishwashing liquid into the water. Using a wooden spoon, agitate the water so that sticky parts peel off. Wait for the water to cool completely to room temperature before proceeding.

Wash crockpot as you would normally do. This should be done immediately after transferring dish into serving bowls/plates.

Conclusion

Thank you again for buying and reading, "*Vegan Instant Pot Cookbook: 5 Ingredients or Less - Quick, Easy, and Healthy Plant Based Meals for Your Family.*"

Although healthy, many people are still hesitant to give vegan food a try. They mistakenly believe that these would be boring, tasteless, and complicated to make. This is the farthest thing from the truth.

Fruits and vegetables are organically delicious, fragrant, and vibrantly colored. If you add herbs, mushrooms, and nuts to the mix, dishes will always come out packed full of flavor. Using mostly whole food (and not highly processed ones,) and with the help of the **Instant Pot**, it only takes a bit of effort and time to prepare great-tasting vegan meals for your family.

This book contains 60+ vegan-safe, easy-to-follow, and affordable recipes for breakfast, lunch, and dinner – along with desserts and savory snack options. Also included are 5-ingredient Homemade Mushroom Stock and Homemade Vegetable Stock –essentials in vegan cooking.

There are also no-cook recipes like: Homemade Coconut Butter, Vegan-Safe Extremely Garlicky Basil Pesto, Homemade Vegan Parmesan Cheese, and a couple of Flavored Vinegar recipes.

This book also contains tips on how to cook certain ingredients for maximum flavor, how to save money while following veganism, and how to use the different functions of the **Instant Pot** properly.

Hopefully, by trying out some of the recipes in this book, you will be encouraged to create your own vegan recipes which you can share with family and friends.

Finally, if you enjoyed this book, then I'd like to ask you for a favor, would you be kind enough to leave a review for this book on Amazon? It'd be greatly appreciated!
Thank you and good luck on your health journey!

Made in the USA
Middletown, DE
27 July 2017